1-20-58

AMERICAN EXPLORATION AND TRAVEL

The Lost Pathfinder
Zebulon Montgomery Pike

The Lost Pathfinder

Zebulon Montgomery Pike

BY W. EUGENE HOLLON

UNIVERSITY OF OKLAHOMA PRESS

NORMAN 1949

To Bette and Suzan

Preface

IN 1803 at the time of the purchase of the Louisiana Territory by the United States, very little was known about the vast region between the Mississippi River and the Rocky Mountains. But in the succeeding decades, explorers, traders, and pioneers gradually dispelled the myth of "The Great American Desert."

Foremost among these explorers was Zebulon Montgomery Pike, for whom the great peak in Colorado was named. Pike spent nineteen of his thirty-four years in the army. (In 1813, during the War of 1812, he was killed at the Battle of York, now Toronto.) He has been called the best brigadier general in the army at the time of his death, but he is principally noticed by historians for his two western expeditions in 1805–1807.

Suspicion has clouded Pike's name for many years because of his friendship for and association with General James Wilkinson. The latter is remembered as the man who betrayed the country to Aaron Burr, and then, his courage failing, betrayed Burr to the country. Pike has been accused of acting as a spy for Wilkinson and Burr, an accusation which, although neither proved nor disproved, has been a blight upon his memory.

I have tried in this volume to weigh impartially such evidence as exists on this phase of his career.

I first became interested in Zebulon Montgomery Pike in 1945 during a conversation with Carl Coke Rister of the University of Oklahoma history staff, who encouraged me to make an investigation of the explorer and his activities.

A generous grant-in-aid from the American Philosophical Society made it possible to search for Pike materials in the Library of Congress and the National Archives, Washington, D. C. A small grant from the Research Council of the University of Oklahoma aided in securing additional materials from several state and private libraries: the Pennsylvania Historical Society Library, Philadelphia; the Chicago Historical Society Library; the University of Texas Archives, Austin; the Mississippi State Archives, Jackson; the University of Kentucky Library, Lexington; the Western Reserve University Library, Cleveland; the Missouri State Historical Society Library, St. Louis; the Louisiana State University Archives, Baton Rouge; and the University of Oklahoma Library.

In addition, materials were obtained from the Pike Family Association, West Newton, Massachusetts, and from various living descendants of the Pike family. I should like to give special thanks to Mrs. Roscoe M. Packard, secretary of the above-mentioned Association.

Among the others who showed an interest in the study and gave valuable leads to materials are Mr. T. R. Hay, Locust Valley, New York; Dr. William R. Hogan, Tulane University, New Orleans; Miss Charlotte Capers, Jackson, Mississippi; Mr. Edwin W. Mills, Osceola, Missouri; Miss Winnie Allen, Austin, Texas; Dr. Ralph Bieber, Washington University, St. Louis; Dr. Paul M. Angle, Chicago Historical Society; Dr. Elizabeth Drewry, National Archives, Washington, D. C.; Mr. George MacReynolds, librarian, Doyleston, Pennsylvania; and Mrs. W. A. Livingston, Fort Dodge, Iowa.

I am deeply grateful to my wife, Bette Francis Hollon, for her help and encouragement. And to my colleagues at the University of Oklahoma, Dr. Carl Coke Rister, Dr. Donnell Owings, Dr. William E. Livezey, and Professor Foster Harris, I extend my thanks for their criticisms and suggestions. Also, I wish to express my appreciation to Mrs. Marcelle B. Richardson and Mrs. Vera L. Esser for typing the manuscript. Errors that inadvertently appear in the narrative are my own.

W. EUGENE HOLLON

Norman, Oklahoma
March 1, 1949

Contents

Illustrations

The Lost Pathfinder
Zebulon Montgomery Pike

I

"A Small Blue Cloud"

IT was November 15, 1806. Lieutenant Zebulon Montgomery Pike and his fifteen companions riding west, clad as they were in thin cotton uniforms, could not ignore the chill winds of eastern Colorado. Winter had come already to the Great Plains. Patches of snow marked the rolling prairie, while herds of buffalo and mustangs forsook their grazing lands.

For several weeks now, their horses half-starved, Pike and his little band of soldiers had ridden farther and farther into this vast and unknown region. Each day had been like the one before. But today would be different: the climax of a stirring life, much of which was yet to be lived.

About two o'clock Pike lifted in his saddle, staring. There on the far western horizon was something that looked like "a small blue cloud." It was gone, and then suddenly there it was again. Only this time it was not a cloud. Rising out of the plains in the northwest towered a tremendous mountain, above a chain of peaks. Now the others saw it, too. With one accord the travelers halted their tired mounts and gave "three cheers to the Mexican Mountains."

Trembling with excitement, the Lieutenant removed his telescope and scanned the peak. He perceived that it was but one of an endless range of mountains extending north and south—the principal chain of the Rockies. Somewhere within these mountains must lie the source of the Arkansas River, an objective of his expedition.

Day after day the party took their course along the winding river, hardships became commonplace, the severity of winter increased, and their horses failed them one by one. On November 23 the travelers halted. "I concluded to put the party in a defensible situation," wrote the Lieutenant in his journal, "and ascend the north fork of the high point [Pike's Peak] of the blue mountains [Front Range] which we conceived would be one day's march, in order to be enabled from its pinacal to lay down the various branches and positions of the country."

The place where Pike built his defensive log stockade lay within the limits of present-day Pueblo. It must have been the first wooden structure erected by an Anglo-American in Colorado. From this place it is fifty miles as the crow flies to the famous peak which now bears the name of its discoverer.

The fortification complete, Lieutenant Pike, Dr. Robinson, and two privates left their companions and struck out on foot for the high point of the mountain range. The "Grand Peak," as Pike called it, now loomed straight ahead, almost due north, and the travelers expected to reach it within a few hours' march. Yet the third day of their journey found them still far from their objective. Between them and the peak appeared a mountain range, the Cheyenne, which had to be surmounted before the base of "Grand Peak" could be reached. When, leaving their baggage and provisions behind, the men began to climb, they found their task more difficult with each successive step. Darkness descended, the cold grew bitter, and they took refuge in a cave.

4

With the morning sun, Pike and his companions, who dragged their weary bodies forth, beheld a panoramic view below them. As he looked back upon the plains whence he had come, Pike remembered that it was Thanksgiving Day (November 27, 1806). "The unbounded prairie was overhung with clouds, which appeared like the ocean in a storm—wave piled on wave and foaming, while the sky was perfectly clear."

At last the mountain at the base of the great peak was conquered. Beyond it towered the enormous mass, its summit crowned with ice and snow. It was as high again as the elevation already ascended and now appeared to be some fifteen or sixteen miles away. An intervening valley, however, made it inaccessible to the exhausted Pike and his companions.

Where they stood, the snow was three feet deep; the thermometer read four degrees below zero. Shivering in his cotton clothes and without stockings on his feet, Pike paused for several minutes and drank in the scenery. "I believe that no human being could have ascended to its pinacal," he later remarked in his journal. Little did he imagine that he was now gazing at his own great monument, literally at the peak of his career. But the tremendous, towering bulk of the giant mountain was impressive enough.

As Lieutenant Pike turned to retrace his steps, he remembered that he and his half-frozen comrades had not eaten for two days. He was not strong either. None of the Pikes were. Even so, it was the tradition of his family, sick or well, to act. He was the second child of Major Zebulon Pike, who fathered a brood of eight. Zebulon Montgomery was also perhaps the sturdiest of the lot. Although he was killed at an early age, he outlived all his brothers and sisters but two. Four of the Pike children died in infancy. The rest, excepting Zebulon Montgomery, were stricken with tuberculosis and either died in

5

youth or lingered into maturity as hopeless invalids. But in Zebulon Montgomery Pike, the restless spirit of the line survived and overcame all handicaps.

The Pikes were prominent under this and variant names; in England as early as the twelfth century, there appear to have been two branches of the family, one in Somerset and the other in Devonshire.

The explorer Pike was descended from the Pikes of Somersetshire, who migrated to London sometime around 1200. John Pike, an attorney, emigrated with his family on the "good ship" *James*, and settled in Ipswich, Massachusetts, in 1635, just seven years after the founding of the old Bay Colony. From Ipswich he moved to Newbury, and later to Salisbury, where he served as a Congregational minister for many years.

John Pike and Sarah Washington, his wife—perhaps a kinswoman of George Washington—had five children, most of whom emigrated to other colonies. One son, Major Robert Pike, remained in Massachusetts and is remembered today because of his refusal to sentence persons accused of witchcraft. Another son, Captain John Pike, the great-great-grandfather of Lieutenant Pike, moved to New Jersey in 1666. He was one of the early settlers of Woodbridge, then a part of Somerset but now in Middlesex County.

Some of the Pikes in Colonial America became famous Indian fighters, others were ministers, sea captains, merchants, magistrates, and councilmen. Zebulon Montgomery's father, Zebulon Pike, was the son of James and Mary Herriot Pike and a great-great-great-grandchild of the first John Pike. He was born on September 18, 1751, at Woodbridge, New Jersey. By the time he had reached the age of ten, both of his parents were dead, leaving the lad a plot of salt upland and meadow in Somerset County.

6

For some years he lived with his maternal grandfather, who subsequently bound him out as apprentice to a saddler. But making harness and saddles was not to his liking. At the first opportunity, Zebulon ran away to sea. He returned to Somerset County as a young man shortly before the American Revolution and served in the Continental Army until the end of the war.

Only a few scattered documents reveal his war experience. On September 11, 1823, he applied for a pension from the federal government under the acts of Congress of March 18, 1818, and May 1, 1820. His signed affidavit is now in the Division of Pension Records in the National Archives.

"The said Zebulon Pike did serve in the Revolutionary War," it states. "He entered into the service of the thirteen United States of America, in the year 1776, as a private volunteer in Captain Haddan's Company of Infantry in the regiment commanded by Col. David Forman in the Jersey line. He served in said regiment during the whole campaign of 1776 during which time he became Quartermaster of said regiment. That in the spring season of the year 1777, he was appointed cornet in a troop of Dragoons, commanded by Capt. More Fontleroy, in Colonel Stephen Moyland's regiment of Dragoons, which after having been sometime raised, was annexed to the Pennsylvania line on the Continental establishment. That he continued to serve in said corps until the close of the war, during which time he was regularly promoted to the ranks of Lieutenant and Captain, to which latter he attained in the year 1778 and bore the same rank until the close of the American Revolutionary War; when he was (with most of the other soldiers of the revolutionary war) finally discharged. He was in the battle of Long Island, White Plains, German-

7

town, and Monmouth, and also in many skirmishes, which the failure of his memory does not now enable him to enumerate."

There is also a letter, signed in Pike's handwriting and addressed to General Anthony Wayne, in the Charles B. Pike Collection at the Chicago Historical Society. Dated July, 1780, it shows that Pike was in Massachusetts at that time, spying on the British Army.

On April 17, 1775, Zebulon Pike married Isabella Brown, the daughter of James Brown of Somerset County, New Jersey. (Brown subsequently became an officer of much distinction during the Revolution, and was a prominent landholder.) Until Zebulon joined the army, he and Isabella lived on a farm in Somerset County. Their first child was born on November 19, 1775, and died nine days later. "Our second child Zebulon was born January 5 in the year 1779," Isabella recorded in the family Bible. This was the son who was destined to become famous. The name "Montgomery" was added some time later, and according to tradition was chosen to honor General Richard Montgomery, who had lost his life in the siege of Quebec. When he was grown, the son almost invariably wrote his signature "Z. M. Pike." But in a last letter to his wife, written a few hours before his death, he affectionately used his middle name, "Montgomery."

Zebulon Montgomery had two brothers and one sister who reached maturity. James Pike lived to be over seventy, but his life was not a happy one. Early afflicted with consumption, he was never able to support himself or his family of eight children. Maria Herriot Pike, the sister and favorite of Zebulon Montgomery, married first Thomas Wardell, a lawyer, and after his death, Anderson Gage. Gage, too, became tubercular and could not take care of his family. The youngest member of the Pike brood, George Washington, reached the age of nineteen before succumbing to the same dread malady that had afflicted all the others.

The exact birthplace of Zebulon Montgomery Pike is in dispute. Most historians maintain that Pike was born in Lamberton, now the southern part of the city of Trenton, in Mercer County, New Jersey. This place has, however, been confused with his real birthplace—Lamberton (now Lamington) in Somerset County. At the time of the American Revolution, the town was called Allamatuck; in 1817 the name was changed to Lamberton, and in 1838 to Lamington. It is located on the east bank of the Lamington River, about two miles northwest of the confluence of that stream and the northern branch of the Raritan River. Now a part of Bedminister Township, Somerset County, it lies immediately east of the line separating that county from Hunterdon.

Soon after Zebulon Pike returned from the Revolutionary War, he removed with his family to Solebury Township in Bucks County, Pennsylvania. Here they settled on a farm originally granted by William Penn in 1705 to one Joseph Pike of Ireland. From Bucks, Zebulon took his family to Northumberland County in the western part of the state, where he bought some land on Bald Eagle Creek, Bald Eagle Township. Their residence here was not prolonged. County records reveal that Captain Zebulon Pike and his wife Isabella deeded to one Jonathan Kinsey 289 acres of land in that county in October, 1786.

Several local historians have tried to prove that Zebulon Montgomery Pike, the explorer, was born in Bucks County, Pennsylvania, and not in New Jersey, but their claim is easily disproved. In the first place, Pike frequently referred to New Jersey as the state of his birth. Then, during the War of 1812

9

he was given the command of the Fifteenth Regiment, a New Jersey corps, an unlikely appointment had he not claimed citizenship in New Jersey, although he had lived there for only a short time during his early youth.

No record of young Pike's school attendance can be found, but he is said to have attended various common schools in western Pennsylvania. According to Elliott Coues,[1] young Pike had private lessons from a Mr. Wall in Bucks County, a mathematician of some local repute. Most of his education, however, was acquired through his own effort and with the help of his father. He was adept in mathematics and later acquired French and Spanish.

In after years Zebulon Montgomery's biographer, General Henry Whiting, described him as "a boy of slender form, very fair complexion, gentle and retiring disposition, but of resolute energies which he readily put to combative test when the occasion arose." Already the child was father to the man. Stubborn and self-willed, his mind reached out toward the unknown with an ambition singularly steadfast. Although many in his day had better limbs and muscles, few, if any, possessed so stout a heart.

[1] The best annotated edition of Pike's journals is that edited by Elliott Coues under the title, *The Expeditions of Zebulon Montgomery Pike.*

2

"Life Was Hard"

THE close of the American Revolution was the signal for a mass migration to the West. Within a few years Kentucky and Tennessee boasted hundreds of settlements—populated for the most part by pioneers from Virginia and North Carolina.

The Ohio country was to be settled principally by immigrants from Pennsylvania and New Jersey. From Pittsburgh the Scotch-Irish migrants in their flat-bottom boats sailed for the new settlements at Cincinnati, North Bend, and other Ohio and Kentucky towns.

Like many small landholders of his place and time, Zebulon Pike felt the urge to leave Pennsylvania for the land of the "Beautiful River," the Ohio, as he observed the daily removal of his friends and neighbors—always going towards the setting sun. But when he first ventured beyond Pittsburgh, it was as a soldier and not as a settler.

Not long after Congress acquired title to the old Northwest, it set itself the task of liquidating the Indian claims in that area. Unhappily the red man failed to grasp the idea of individual ownership. To the Indian, it was as wrong for an individual to lay claim to a plot of land as to appropriate all of the animals of the forest or the water in the streams. He fought back in the tradition of his race; and the frontier villages, feeling the brunt of these attacks, now appealed to the federal government for protection.

As Indian treaties were broken as soon as they were made, some sterner action was evidently necessary. Therefore, in 1790 Congress empowered President Washington to call out the militias of Kentucky, Virginia, and Pennsylvania for frontier defense. General Josiah Harmar, already stationed at Fort Washington (Cincinnati) with 140 regulars, was the logical choice for their commander.

The result of Harmar's campaign is well known. He tried desperately and vainly to drill his motley crew of fifteen hundred militia and regulars into an effective army. Ambushed about one hundred miles north of Cincinnati, almost two hundred of his men were scalped, while scores more were injured. Harmar was forced to make a humiliating retreat. Some of his "riff-raff" were so stricken with terror that they did not halt their flight until they reached Fort Washington.

The Indians continued their depredations with increased boldness. Panic reigned among the frontier people. Another campaign was essential, and for it additional troops must be raised and competent officers found. Zebulon Pike, now forty years of age, responded to the call and received a captaincy in the Pennsylvania militia. His pay was thirty-five dollars a month, with twelve dollars subsistence.

Privates were enlisted at $2.10 for each month's service. Most of them were recruited from the jails and poorhouses in the East, while others volunteered merely to go West, expecting there to desert and squat on public land. For the most part, indeed, this second expedition was made up of aimless, ignorant, shiftless drifters, men with little sense of responsibility.

This time Washington felt compelled to place General Arthur St. Clair, governor of the Ohio Territory, in command of the three thousand troops being raised. St. Clair, already at Cincinnati, ordered the newly appointed officers to receive the recruits at Pittsburgh, organize them into companies, and deliver them in barges as quickly as possible.

Captain Zebulon Pike, whose company was the eighth corps to be organized and to embark from Pittsburgh, reached Fort Washington on August 26, 1791, after a river journey of eleven weeks.

By September, General St. Clair had here gathered a force of two thousand non-commissioned officers and men. As most of them were militia troops, they were little better prepared for an Indian campaign than the army under Harmar. They were "badly clothed, badly fed, and badly paid." Many brought along their wives or mistresses.

According to James Ripley Jacobs, these women "were not beautiful and virtue was not one of their strong points. . . . Had they not been strong," he continues, "they could never have survived the hardships that they suffered. Like the frontier, they were rough in language and action; their conversation was often shot through with profanity, their conduct earthy and unregenerate. They suffered stoically and when necessary they would, and did fight bravely."[1] But to Captain Pike these camp followers were a disgrace to the army. He felt only disgust for the men who fought over them and who frequently were unable to fight because of them.

The plan of attack which General St. Clair had devised was based upon the construction of a series of forts from Cincinnati, north along the Miami River, to Lake Erie. Building them, however, was the worst sort of drudgery and played

[1] James Ripley Jacobs, *The Beginnings of the U. S. Army, 1783–1812*, 90.

havoc with the morale of the men. More than five hundred deserted within the first six months, leaving their officers with less than fourteen hundred troops to continue the campaign.

By the end of September, 1791, three of the forts had been completed, and the main body of the army had encamped on the Wabash not far from present Greenville, Ohio. There, on November 4, just as the men were being dismissed from parade, the Indians made a surprise attack. Within a few minutes the Americans were surrounded by howling savages who fired their guns and arrows with notable accuracy.

The fighting began about half an hour before sunrise. At first the soldiers could not see the enemy, who were well concealed against the surrounding forests, while they were themselves excellent targets. In the prevailing confusion it was difficult for the officers to enforce orders. Some companies, however, did manage to form and to make a creditable showing. The battle lasted for almost four hours before a general retreat was ordered. Most of the high-ranking officers, including General St. Clair, remained cool and deliberate through the entire fray. But with few exceptions the militia behaved "like a lot of shameless cowards." Many of the women, on the other hand, fought bravely, and all but three out of some two hundred of them were butchered and their bodies mutilated.

Captain Pike's company, attached to General Richard Butler's regiment, bore the first shock and suffered heavily throughout the fray. It is reported that their general, who received a wound in the arm and body shortly after the fighting began, summoned Captain Pike to his side and said: "I cannot live; you load my pistol and set me against a tree, and I will die fighting, and you will tell my friends so." General Butler was killed a few minutes later. The savages cut out his heart and ate it, hoping to acquire thereby a little of his valor.

By nine o'clock, General St. Clair felt obliged to order a retreat. Some of the troops then managed to cut their way out of the encirclement and effect a withdrawal, the Indians pursuing them for two or three miles before returning to kill the wounded and collect the booty. The savages danced and howled at the screams of their prisoners. Some of the unfortunates were roasted at the stake. "They pulled out men's intestines bit by bit," General St. Clair wrote to the Secretary of War. "They flayed others alive and slowly hacked or wrenched their limbs away. They dashed out the brains of children against the trunks of trees and flung their battered bodies into the brush. Some of the women were stretched naked upon the ground and run through with wooden stakes; others were cut in two after their breasts had been hacked away."[2]

Those who managed to escape continued their flight until they reached Fort Jefferson, almost thirty miles away. Captain Pike, now in command of what was left of General Butler's regiment, managed to keep his head. Calling his troops around him, he told them that their lives depended upon their staying together and obeying orders. He had them load their guns on the run and stop and shoot at the pursuing enemy only when so ordered.

The younger men had a good chance to escape. But Captain Pike, who had suffered a partial paralysis several years before, now found that his legs would not carry him to safety. Seized with severe cramps and forced to stop, he ordered his troops to continue their retreat until they reached the fort.

As he rested upon a log, Pike saw his friend Dr. Ellison, an army surgeon, and a young boy retreating on a wounded horse. "Don't just sit there and be butchered by these devils," Ellison shouted. "Take hold of my horse's mane and perhaps

[2] *Ibid.*, 110.

the cramps will leave you." Pike grabbed the mane and hobbled along beside the animal until his legs became stronger. The wounded horse carried the two men and the boy safely to Fort Jefferson. Dr. Ellison, who later settled in Cincinnati, where he practiced medicine for many years, rewarded his faithful mount by turning him out to pasture.

President Washington was much chagrined over this new disaster. The country was aroused and demanded revenge. And the Indians of the Northwest, taunting the Americans to come and take the land north of the Ohio, continued their reckless plundering.

It was generally recognized that militia was no longer sufficient. Regulars who were well trained and ably led would be needed to salvage the country's prestige and make the West safe for its pioneers. Therefore, Congress, on March 5, 1792, provided for a regular force of 5,120 officers and men. This new army would constitute a legion, to be divided into four sub-legions of 1,280 men each—consisting of one troop of dragoons, one company of artillery, four companies of riflemen, and eight companies of infantry.[3]

Washington's first choice for a new commander-in-chief was "Light Horse" Harry Lee, father of the future Confederate general. However, Congress objected to Lee because it felt that already too many high officials of the government were from Virginia. Thus the command went to "Mad Anthony" Wayne, a veteran of eight years' service in the Revolution and the hero of several important skirmishes. Wayne proceeded to Philadelphia immediately and commenced the task of raising three-year enlistments.

Zebulon Pike, who found it increasingly difficult to support a growing family on his Pennsylvania land, decided to

[3] *American State Papers, Military Affairs*, I, 41.

LIEUTENANT ZEBULON MONTGOMERY PIKE

join the new regular army. On March 5, 1792, the day Congress passed the bill to increase the armed forces, he obtained a commission as captain. General Wayne at first ordered him to report to Trenton, New Jersey, and supervise the recruiting service in that area, but on September 4, Pike was assigned to the Third Sub-Legion and transferred to Pittsburgh.

General Wayne did not intend to repeat the mistakes of his predecessors. He moved his newly gathered army of twenty-five hundred troops from Pittsburgh to a temporary encampment below the city on the Ohio River. Legionville, as the new post was called, soon became the scene of intense activity. Officers were instructed by the commander to set an example of neatness and conduct. Enlisted men who committed minor offenses were to be punished by three "duckings" in the icy waters of the Ohio. Major violators were to be dealt with more harshly—usually one hundred lashes on the bare back. There was occasional resort to capital punishment.

Within a few months the troops at Legionville were molded into an effective fighting force. They were trained in close-order drill and were taught to shoot at objects rather than to fire in volleys as had been the custom. Officers were made to apply themselves, and sloven companies got fatigue until they improved.

In April, 1793, Wayne's army began its move down the Ohio to Fort Washington. Most of the officers took their families with them. Others brought along their concubines. The camp followers and "washerwomen" came of their own accord. Captain Pike's family now consisted of his wife, three sons, and a daughter. Zebulon Montgomery was fourteen years of age, James was eight, Maria Herriot was four, and George Washington, the youngest, was born on April 7, a few weeks before the family sailed for Cincinnati.

As the barges laden with soldiers, supplies, women, and children neared Cincinnati, the town turned out one thousand strong to welcome them. General Wayne selected a camp site about one mile west of Fort Washington. This post, which had been manned with one company left over from St. Clair's army, was commanded by that "nefarious gentlemen and soldier," General James Wilkinson.

Wilkinson was a man about whom trouble always gathered. Vain, bombastic, and incompetent, he was constantly obliged to defend his "honor" against the charges of a host of enemies. He was a master of petty treasons, with a gift for scandal. Later he planned to betray the country to Aaron Burr, but, his courage failing, he betrayed Burr to the country instead.

Little did young Zebulon Montgomery Pike realize in 1793 how completely his career would be linked with that of the specious General. To the boy of fourteen, Wilkinson was a gallant leader, a dashing Indian fighter, a hero of the Revolution. It was an image that Pike, the famous explorer, never forgot. Indeed, his friendship for this flamboyant man is a paradox in the otherwise unblemished life of Zebulon Montgomery Pike.

Wilkinson's chief duty in the Northwest was to pacify the Indians, if he could. Meantime, he was to lay in a supply of food and equipment at the various forts, pending the arrival of Wayne's army. The new commander-in-chief's regard for Wilkinson was slight. The feeling was returned in kind.

Fort Washington, Wilkinson's headquarters until 1793, was small, housing only 150 men, more or less. It was located in the frontier village of Cincinnati, whose Scotch-Irish settlers were generous but crude, hospitable but easily aroused, imbibing liquor and frontier religion with equal gusto. It was here that Zebulon Pike and his family lived for the next year and a half. During this time, Captain Pike was commander of the post.

Life at a frontier outpost in 1793 proved to be hard, ugly and brutal; but the Pike children soon became accustomed to it. Isabella Pike tended her brood and watched over her garden of beans and okra outside the log walls of the stockade. Here, too, she saw her eldest son grow into maturity. For in 1794, Zebulon Montgomery, aged fifteen, was already a man and fit for man's work. He enlisted in the army and was at first attached to his father's company, but within a short time he joined Wayne's troops in the northern wilderness.

There, in the opening months of 1794, General Wayne's forces moved north and constructed Fort Recovery amid the bones of St. Clair's fallen army. Fort Defiance, deep in the heart of the Indian country, was completed before the end of the following summer. The Indians, alarmed at this penetration of their hunting grounds, determined to stop the advance before it was too late.

On August 20, 1794, occurred the Battle of Fallen Timbers. The site of this engagement was a few miles north of Fort Defiance at a place where the trees had recently been felled by a terrific storm. Here for about forty-five minutes, one thousand American troops engaged five hundred Indian warriors. The Americans lost thirty-three men to only nineteen of the enemy. But the Indians, perceiving they had no chance against good troops and well-manned stockades, withdrew from the battle and dared not renew the fight.

General Wayne repaired to Fort Greenville as the winter months approached. Time now was against the Indians. Driven from their cornfields and hunting grounds, they shortly faced starvation, while their British allies in Canada ceased to heed their pleas for food and military aid.

On August 3, 1795, the Treaty of Greenville was signed, whereby the Indians gave up their Ohio country and parts of eastern Indiana. Settlers along the Ohio River were overjoyed with their new-found security, and once again the way was open to westward migrants.

The forts Wayne had constructed were to be occupied by troops for several months. To young Zebulon Montgomery Pike fell the task of transporting supplies from Fort Washington to the various garrisons along the Miami River. These supplies were carried in barges as far as the river was navigable, and thence along the wilderness roads to the various forts extending like a chain all the way to Fort Detroit.

We are uncertain whether Pike himself fought at the Battle of Fallen Timbers, although in a letter to the Secretary of War he does make this claim. No account of his experiences in that engagement has been found, and his subsequent correspondence implies that he did not actually meet the enemy in combat.

3

"Never . . . a Slave to Any Man"

SOON after the Indians of the Ohio country had been subdued, young Zebulon Montgomery Pike was sent to join his father, under orders of September 2, 1795, on what was then the far western frontier. "You are to proceed with all possible dispatch for Fort Washington," wrote General Wayne, "from whence you will descend the Ohio with the same barge and crew (who are to receive and obey your orders) with which you ascend, and deliver the dispatches and stores committed to your charges to Captain Pike, commandant of Fort Massac—taking his receipt for same."[1]

Captain Pike had been put in charge of this post in the same year. Erected under Wayne's orders in 1794, it stood on the north bank of the Ohio some forty miles east of the Mississippi, on the site of an old French fort abandoned after the French and Indian War. Its mission was to protect the western pioneers and to inspect river traffic moving from the Ohio to the Mississippi. It formed, moreover, one link in a chain of such military posts extending eventually all the way from Pittsburgh to the Gulf.

Although the Indians here were no longer the menace

[1] Wayne to Z. M. Pike, September 2, 1795, Charles B. Pike Collection, Chicago Historical Society.

they had been, pioneers now scented danger from another source. Spain, possessor of the Gulf Coast and the mouth of the Mississippi, seemed determined to halt an American advance which threatened her northeastern provinces. Westward migrants were equally determined to settle the country. There had been much talk of filibustering expeditions from Ohio and Kentucky, and these, if realized, might end the uneasy peace. So it became part of the duty of Captain Pike and his little force to inspect all barges down the Ohio, thwarting the filibusters before they could do their mischief.

In 1798, Captain Pike was made assistant quartermaster of Fort Pickering, near present Memphis, Tennessee, of which post he received command, with the rank of major, in March, 1800. Some months thereafter he returned to Fort Massac, from which he transferred in 1803 to Fort Wayne, Indiana. His military career was now near its close, for advancing years had greatly enfeebled him and were soon to render him unfit for responsible command. After a brief and probably unsuccessful experiment in school teaching at Lawrenceburg, Indiana, Major Pike retired to his farm in Dearborn County in 1805. Here he remained until his death in 1834, except for a brief period during the War of 1812. At that time he was brevetted a lieutenant colonel, but apparently was unable to perform any military service. An indulgent government continued his salary until 1815.

In the early years of Captain Pike's command at Fort Massac, young Zebulon Montgomery was attached to his father's company. The younger Pike's experience in General Wayne's campaign of 1794–95, carrying supplies to the military posts of the Northwest, could now be put to use. During most of the next five years, he distributed commodities to the forts along the Ohio and the Mississippi.

22

These supplies were furnished through private contractors. River barges, which could then reach most of the western forts, would take on cargoes at Pittsburgh or Cincinnati and float down the Ohio, discharging their goods en route. Young Pike was able to supplement his income by acting as an agent for the contractors. Frequently he commanded as many as twelve boats at a time, each manned by a crew numbering from five to ten men. He matured rapidly, developing the qualities of leadership and responsibility of a man much older than his years.

On one of these Ohio voyages Pike's ability to maintain command was put to test. This particular morning found the weather very cold and the river full of ice. As he prepared to embark, Pike noticed that practically all seventy of the soldiers were scrambling into the two smaller craft, trying to evade the heavier duty of poling and rowing the larger vessels. Furious, Pike whirled to the nearest campfire and bombarded the struggling men with flaming chunks of wood. It was literally trial by fire, and order was restored instantly. After that there was no doubt who was in command, and no further trouble was encountered.

On March 3, 1799, Pike was made a second lieutenant, and on November 1 of that year, a first lieutenant. He was now attached to the First Infantry Regiment and was stationed at Fort Allegheny in western Pennsylvania. A companion who knew him during these formative years has left a telling description. One perceives that Pike was a zealous and efficient soldier with a polished manner and an inquisitive mind. He was strong willed, often stoical, but always courteous, except when aroused to righteous indignation.

"His appearance was military, yet somewhat peculiar; he generally leaned or inclined his head to one side so that the

23

tip of his chapeau touched the right shoulder on parade. His stature was about five feet eight inches, tolerably square and robust for his age. . . . His complexion was ruddy, eyes blue, light hair, and features good. His habits were in keeping with his character, uniformly abstentious and temperate; his attention to duty unremitting. He was a tolerable good English scholar and wrote a good hand . . . and also acquired by his own persevering industry a tolerably good knowledge of the French language."[2]

As a young man, Pike showed great physical endurance. He enjoyed outdoor sports and was particularly fond of hunting and fishing. Few could match his skill as a marksman. He had broad shoulders, but his face was somewhat delicate: his hair light and wavy, eyes deep-set, mouth large, and nose acquiline. In the language of his day, he was "tolerably handsome."

A story told about Lieutenant Pike during his stay at Fort Allegheny, around 1800, reveals both his good and his bad qualities as a man. Extremely temperate himself, Pike did not hesitate to punish subordinates who drank and caroused. Late one evening he and a fellow officer, returning to camp from Pittsburgh, decided to conceal themselves in the brush near camp and catch some of the troops suspected of drinking and "wenching."

They were not disappointed. Sounds from the camp left little doubt of the men's riotous behavior. Suddenly Pike and his companion dashed from their place of concealment and caught the soldiers by surprise. Many tried to run away and escape recognition, but most were caught and punished.

---

[2] General John R. Williams to Major Amos Holton, Detroit, May 20, 1845, quoted in Coues, *op. cit., xxiv.*

Early in 1801 Lieutenant Pike supervised the building of a new fort, or cantonment, a few miles below Fort Massac, called Wilkinsonville, in honor of General Wilkinson, then commander of the army. Here troops could be quartered pending their transfer to posts in construction along the Mississippi, since Fort Massac was too small to accommodate them.

At this place Pike assumed the duties of adjutant of the corps. His work was arduous and unremitting. In addition to regular guard and police duty, there was battalion drill two or three times a week. Company drill was required every day, and the officers themselves drilled once or twice a week. Undoubtedly Pike had valuable experience at Wilkinsonville. His fellow officers, all of whom had served under General Wayne in 1794–95, were probably the best in the army. Some of them were later prominent in the War of 1812, and one became a famous explorer—Meriwether Lewis.

Despite the long hours spent in drill and the routine duties of an adjutant, Lieutenant Pike found time to improve his mind. At night he spent many hours in the study of mathematics and French, and later Spanish. The knowledge thus acquired, combined with his experience as a leader of men, provide one reason for his being chosen to explore parts of the Louisiana Territory in later years.

One of the young lieutenant's favorite books was Robert Dodsley's *Economy of Human Life,* and since he read it many times, the work must have played no small part in shaping his own philosophy. It seems to have colored, too, the language of his correspondence. Incidentally, Pike presented his own copy of the *Economy of Human Life* to his wife shortly after their marriage. Mrs. Pike apparently treasured the book as long as she lived. It was destroyed by fire around 1890, along with most of Pike's personal papers.

On his many trips up and down the Ohio River from 1795 to 1801, Lieutenant Pike soon came to know several of the farmers and planters in Kentucky and the Ohio country. He sometimes visited in their homes, enjoyed their hospitality, and purchased supplies for the various frontier forts. One of Pike's regular stops was at the Brown plantation near Sugar Grove, Kentucky. This small settlement was on the Ohio River about fifteen miles below Cincinnati. Captain John Brown, formerly of Somerset County, New Jersey, had settled here soon after the Revolution, and before his death in 1789 had accumulated a good estate with several dozen slaves. His son and heir, Captain James Brown, was Lieutenant Pike's maternal uncle.

Young Pike became attached to his cousin, Clarissa Brown, in the course of his frequent stops at Sugar Grove. It was not long before the two were corresponding, and soon they made plans to be married. Clarissa, or Clara as Pike always called her, was eighteen years of age in 1801. In later years she was described as tall, dignified, rather austere, and always dressed in black. She usually wore a large, dark crepe shawl over her shoulders and a black crepe turban on her head. For a woman of her day, she was very well educated. She read French fluently and kept a diary in that language for many years. Unfortunately, this journal was destroyed in the same fire as her husband's papers in 1890.

It was a love match, this engagement between the dashing Lieutenant and the shy plantation girl. But her father was obstinate and domineering, and when Pike came to Sugar Grove in 1801 to ask his cousin's hand, Captain Brown refused. The young couple eloped to Cincinnati, where they were married, and lived there for some months during Pike's service at Fort Washington.

Captain Brown, a man who nursed resentments, now wrote to Major Zebulon Pike about his son's behavior. Judging from subsequent correspondence, the Major and his family journeyed to Sugar Grove to hear Brown's story, and Major Pike then wrote to his son at Cincinnati.

"The concern you express for fear I should subject myself to censure below," young Pike replied, "I feel myself undelected to the sentiments from which they flow. But at the same time I feel no consuous of the propriety of my public conduct since at this place, that I am equally willing it should become the object of public investigation and private scrutiny. For as certain as the meridian sun dissipates the morning vapor, so would the clearness of my official character dispell the dark insinuations pointed against me, either by open enemies or individious friends.

"With respect to my conduct in connection with Captain Brown, it may possible be a little too independent where my private situation is taken into view. But although I have thought my folly and extravagance in youth forfeited in a degree my independence of situation, still nothing can justify an unconditional submission to the will of any man in existence, and should I be confined to the walls of a prison, still shouldn't my soul be free; and scorn to ask assistance of any man who will grant it or act, agreeable to my own will and the laws of my country.

"At the same time I will willingly receive the advise of those either my superior in rank, age, or connected with me by ponsanguinity [*sic*]—sensible that youth is subject to errors and wants the cool and correct judgment of age to correct their over-heated immigination; but whilst I have the breath *I will never be the slave of any man* [*italics mine*] whilst he

27

thinks that his authority is derived from pecuniary motive, but from gratitude he might expect great sacrifices."[3]

In many respects this letter is a mirror of Lieutenant Pike's character. He was independent and headstrong, and he had a mind of his own. Much of his subsequent correspondence reveals the same lofty sense of honor not untainted with self-righteousness. Ordinarily Pike was not a vindictive person. Although there is no evidence that he ever visited his father-in-law after 1801, he later referred to him frequently in letters to his parents and relatives. In 1803, Pike wrote to his young sister, Maria, "Mama informs me she and Captain Brown have disputed; for this I am sorry, but shall write Mama on the subject."

In 1812, Pike, then a colonel, wrote from Philadelphia to one of his aunts, Mrs. Jeanet Pike Gage, that "Captain Brown is very rich, worth about 150,000 dollars, but as yet I have benefited by it but little, but being obliged to live in a style that costs me from two to three thousand dollars per annum, I find myself scarce enough of money."[4] The pay for a colonel in the army in 1812 amounted to approximately $1,500, including subsistence.

When Captain Brown died in 1824, his plantation passed to his daughter, Clara Pike. At that time she was living with her daughter and son-in-law in Vincennes, Indiana. She subsequently returned to Sugar Grove, her daughter's family moving with her, and managed the estate until her death in 1847.

[3] Z. M. Pike to Zebulon Pike, Western Reserve Historical Society, Archives, Cleveland.

[4] Z. M. Pike to Mrs. Jeanet Pike Gage, Pike Family Association, West Newton, Massachusetts.

The graves of Pike's wife and daughter, in the old family burial ground of the Brown plantation, were untended for decades. In the late nineteen twenties the Daughters of the American Revolution erected a monument on the site, and provisions have since been made for the upkeep of the plot. The cemetery is in sight of the Ohio River, not far from the great power plant of the Columbia Gas and Electric Company.

4

"Other Services . . . in View"

LIEUTENANT PIKE and his young wife lived at Fort Washington from late 1801 until the summer of 1802, but since he continued as agent for the contractors, he was frequently away from the post. On one occasion, indeed, he journeyed to Washington, carrying dispatches for General Wilkinson. Crude as it still was, the federal capital must have offered a striking contrast to the raw frontier post. And certainly Pike would notice it.

The Lieutenant was in fact dubious about remaining in the army all the rest of his life; yet he had not chosen any other profession. His station at Cincinnati was not undesirable, and he might have been satisfied to remain there, or perhaps eventually to take a staff appointment in the East. But as luck would have it, he was now to be attached to the First Infantry Regiment and ordered yet farther west, even to the outermost fringe of civilization.

Pike, however, accepted his new assignment with good grace, remembering perhaps what excellent chances for promotion accompanied frontier service. Already the flood of pioneers was spilling over into Indiana. These people had to be protected from the Indians, and, like the branches of an ever growing vine, the chain of forts moved westward with

30

the settlers. Sometimes these military posts appeared beyond the farthest settlements, and sometimes well behind. Usually the troops and the civilians kept pace with each other.

The earlier frontier forts sprang up along the banks of the Ohio and other rivers of the West, but later establishments might be found deep in the backwoods on less important streams. Such a place was Fort Knox, on the banks of the Wabash at the old French settlement of Vincennes. And to this post came Zebulon Montgomery and Clara Pike in the summer of 1802.

Vincennes proved to be a most depressing place—a mean-looking village on a flat prairie near the river. The low banks were covered with weeds, rotten from the floods of spring. The water was contaminated, and the air stank. This section of Indiana was a raw, wet country, winter and spring. Although the land near Vincennes was fertile enough, the French settlers had made little effort to cultivate it. They were described by a traveler a few years following Pike's stay as "low, ignorant, and superstitious."[1] Many of them were turbulent and shiftless "squaw-men." Some wore breechcloths like their brothers in the forest. Their lodges gathered filth, their bodies dirt and vermin.[2]

The French had settled this place by 1736 as part of an effort to hold the Old Northwest against the English. For many years it had been called "Old Post," a corruption of the French *au poste*, but eventually its name became Vincennes

---

[1] Maximilian, Prince of Wied, *Travels in the Interior of North America*, in Reuben Gold Thwaites (ed.), *Early Western Travels, 1748–1846*, XXIV, 137.

[2] In 1765 the British Indian Agent, George Croghan, visited Vincennes. "The French inhabitants hereabouts," he wrote in his journal, "are an idle, lazy people, a parcel of renegades from Canada, and are much worse than the Indians." See *A Selection of George Croghan's Letters and Journals*, in Thwaites, *Early Western Travels*, I, 141.

in honor of one François Margane, Sieur de Vincennes, who had campaigned against the neighboring Indians. For many decades its population rarely exceeded forty or fifty families.

In 1763 the French lost the region south of the Great Lakes to the British, who were slow to garrison the former military posts. And in 1778 the intrepid George Rogers Clark captured Vincennes. When the American Revolution ended five years later, the United States withdrew its troops and did not reoccupy the fort until after 1800. By this time many Americans had arrived and settled.

The first English-speaking pioneers were little better prepared than the natives; some were unsavory characters whose crimes had driven them to the frontier. Others were dissipated young men unable to live at home—the backwash of civilized society.

By 1800 the population of the Indiana country justified its organization into a separate territory with William Henry Harrison as governor.[3] Vincennes was chosen for the capital, and for a time its future seemed assured. The log cabins of the French now began to yield to the clapboard houses of the Scotch-Irish. Coonskin caps and buckskin shirts, the badges of the frontier, appeared less frequently, the linsey-woolsey garments of traders and farmers more often.

By the time Lieutenant Pike arrived, the townspeople had erected a school building; a sawmill was in operation turning out cut-lumber for new houses; and the local tavern did a thriving business. Still the settlement left much to be desired.

Pike and his wife now took up quarters inside Fort Knox. It was a relatively small post, built of logs in the form of a

[3] Governor Harrison erected a brick mansion at Vincennes in 1805. It was the first building of its kind in the Northwest, and the estate was long noted for its beautiful gardens and grounds. Later it became the home of Zebulon Montgomery Pike's widow and daughter.

View of Cincinnati
in the early nineteenth century

Fort Sackville (Vincennes), 1779
renamed Fort Knox before 1800

quadrangle and housing about one hundred troops with the officers and their families. The principal buildings were constructed inside the quadrangle against the walls, while a parade ground occupied the center. Officers' quarters, barracks, post traders' establishments, and a hospital were all together on one side. Opposite were the stables, quartermaster's supplies, and a store room. A guard house, company kitchen, workshops, and laundry occupied the other two sides of the quadrangle.

Life at Fort Knox, though sometimes pleasant, was more often merely boring. The officers and their wives, a tight little clique, maintained the standards of the East as far as they could, enjoying such luxuries as were brought up the river in wet seasons. In dry seasons supplies had to come by ox and mule train or by pack horse.

With the officers and their families living so close together, petty feuds and jealousies were a natural consequence. Rarely did a man's personal life escape the curious eyes of his neighbor. When weather permitted, parties went horseback riding or hunting. At other times they played cards, danced, or enjoyed the social games of the time. And in the spring they worked their small gardens outside the walls of the fort.

With low pay and little activity, enlisted men found much to grumble at. Lonely and bored, they too often lay with Indian women and camp followers. Desertions were common, and punishment for the least offense severe. Drinking, gambling, and fighting seemed to be part of army life—much to Lieutenant Pike's disgust.

Occasionally, however, troops were called out to escort a body of pioneers through the backwoods or to protect surveyors from the Indians. Sometimes roads and trails had to be cut through the forests, bridges constructed, river navigation guarded, and supplies hauled back to the fort.

33

Away from the post, men found conditions yet more depressing. Their food was coarse, consisting mostly of wild game when it was available. Often they slept on the wet ground, without covering and in constant danger of Indian attack. On such occasions they secretly cursed the army and its officers and more openly themselves for becoming soldiers. When they returned to the fort, however, they sometimes got a few days' rest, with extra rations of whiskey, as a reward for their labors.

Lieutenant Pike gave most of his spare time to the pursuit of learning. He continued his studies, unlike most of his fellow officers, becoming proficient in Spanish and French and in elementary science.

During his tour of duty at Vincennes, and later at Kaskaskia, Pike wrote often to his parents and to his brothers and sister. Fortunately some of these letters have survived, a dozen or more being among the archives of Western Reserve University. From them a glimpse of the personal feelings and ambitions of the young officer in these years is obtained.

Very soon after reaching his new post on the frontier of Indiana, Pike observed in a letter to his father dated February 28, 1802: "I can scarcely obtain time between the duties of my station and the company and amusements of the Governor and other families, as the military are all the vogue, to write to you in day light."[4]

Indeed, the Lieutenant and the very popular Governor Harrison,[5] later the "hero of Tippecanoe" and subsequently

[4] Unless otherwise indicated, all of Pike's correspondence to members of his family from 1801 to 1803, and herein quoted, are taken from original letters now in the possession of the Western Reserve Historical Society, Cleveland. A more complete statement concerning these documents is found in the bibliography, pages 219–20.

[5] Gerald W. Johnson *(American Heroes and Hero-Worship,* 112) recently

34

ninth president of the United States, soon became warm friends. The family bond was later further cemented when Harrison's oldest son, John Cleves Symmes Harrison, married Pike's only surviving child, Clarissa.

At another time Pike was distressed with his situation and with army life in general. President Jefferson, seeing in the regular army a danger to the new republic and a needless expense to the people, wanted to reduce its number to the barest minimum. Lieutenant Pike had learned of a bill for reorganizing the armed forces, and his uneasiness is reflected in another letter to his father, whose strength by now was spent.

"You will perceive of the late bill (which I have no doubt ere this, is passed into law), that agreeable to all human probability you will be disbanded—and notwithstanding the motion made by General Smith and the still more noble one of the Honorable W. Griswood to provide for those who have grown grey in the service of their country. You are to be dismissed with the noble and adequate provision of three whole month's pay and subsistence. Wonderful indeed in the present race for economy. That's the ending for a man who had bled and spent his youth in the service of an ungrateful country— fine encouragement for the sons to tred in the footsteps of their father.

"Unless I can obtain one of the profitable and honorable

observed: "William Henry Harrison, probably an honest man, and certainly not a subtle one, is one of the most contradictory figures in American history. It was Harrison's singular fate to lose money when he worked hard and intelligently, to grow rich when he gambled recklessly, to be loaded with praise when he engaged in dubious enterprises, to be damned for a traitor when he won the country's battles, to be scorned for what he was, and to be exalted to the skies for what he emphatically was not. Admittedly ignorant of politics, he beat the master politicians who had beaten Clay, Webster, and Calhoun. After a long career of frustration, disappointment, and bitterness, he was suddenly elevated to the very summit of political ambition—and it promptly killed him."

35

staff appointments contemplated in the bill, I have other services shortly in view, but my plan must be matured and foundation sure. [Pike apparently thought of becoming a private contractor to furnish supplies to the army—a very lucrative business, judging from the wealth of some who followed it.]

". . . My dear sir, believe that I feel the ties of duty and inclination much closer drawn from the idea of your embarrassment and without immediate profession would sacrifice much of my future prospects and inclinations if I could by that smooth the decline of life of my parents.

". . . Where is James, Marie, and George. When I think of them, my duty seems to make me the more forceable to quit the army."[6]

Throughout his short adult life, Pike kept in close touch with his parents, brothers, and sister. More and more they depended on him for advice and solace and wrote to him of their hardships and sorrows.

To his thirteen-year-old sister, Marie, Pike wrote on November 22, 1803: "I console you on the solitary situation in which you are placed, but hope that it may be the course of the improvement of your mind, the graces of which shines in the countenance and beautifies the body. You should employ what leisure time you can command in reading and writing. Your words are generally pretty well spelt, but the writing is bad. Practice more and learn to write without quite so much flourish."

At another time,[7] the Lieutenant advised his sister further on the subject of her education: "Your letter is wrote well with respect to language, but it is too much crowded and wants a

[6] Zebulon Montgomery Pike to Zebulon Pike, February 28, 1802, Western Reserve Historical Society Archives.

[7] February 6, 1803.

little more attention in the stops—Again let me entreat your attention Maria to the cultivation of your mind—for not youth alone, but a long life, is all too little to acquire the art of learning."

A self-taught man, Pike, more than other men, knew the value of learning, and he constantly reminded his young sister and two brothers of their need for education. He particularly wanted his younger brother, ten-year-old George Washington Pike, to study and become an officer, advising his parents to send the boy to a private tutor in Detroit. Unfortunately the lad was a poor student, his interests and thoughts far removed from his studies. "Unless you make rapid advances in learning, for the time you are lost," chided Zebulon Montgomery. Doubtless to the satisfaction of his brother, George later was admitted to the United States Military Academy at West Point in 1809.

The situation of James Brown Pike, five years younger than Zebulon Montgomery, already seemed hopeless. James had been stricken with tuberculosis in childhood, and his death was now yearly expected; but, ironically, he survived all of his brothers and sisters. He went through life, however, without even an elementary education and could follow no gainful pursuit. Lieutenant Pike often mentioned James in letters to the family, always in a spirit of pity and sadness.

Early in 1803 Pike was transferred farther west. Already the finger tips of civilization were feeling out the Illinois country, and once again forts followed in the wake of pioneers, bringing a semblance of permanence and stability to the ever moving frontier.

One hundred and fifty miles west of Vincennes lay Kaskaskia, another French town of similar history. In 1703 the Jesuits had established a mission on the Kaskaskia River, six miles above its confluence with the Mississippi; and although the mission did not flourish, the settlement around it managed to survive. In 1723 it boasted twelve white people and a number of Indians. The French had built a fort here in 1736, only to lose it to the British in the French and Indian War. Renamed Fort Gage by the British, it was in turn captured by George Rogers Clark in the American Revolution and had but recently been regarrisoned.

When Pike arrived at Kaskaskia, the settlement contained forty or fifty families. André Michaux, a French traveler and filibuster, described the place as it looked about 1800.

"Nothing is to be seen but houses in ruins and abandoned because the French of the Illinois country, having always been brought up in and accustomed to the fur trade with the savages, have become the laziest and most ignorant of all men," Michaux wrote. "They live and the majority of them are clothed in the manner of the savages. They wear no breeches but pass between their thighs a piece of cloth of about one third of an ell (in length) which is kept in place before and behind above the hips by a belt."[8]

On the coming of American troops in 1803, the town had begun to grow. Within a year its population had risen to seventy or eighty permanent families, not counting soldiers. Its location gave easy access to the port of New Orleans, and few settlements in the Far West could boast better commercial possibilities. A land office was soon opened, a post office established, and, not long afterward, a school. A second tavern now appeared to accommodate the growing number of boatmen, hunters, traders, and trappers passing through.

Yet despite its nearness to the Mississippi, Kaskaskia con-

---

[8] André Michaux, *Journal of Travels into Kentucky, 1793–1796*, in Thwaites, *Early Western Travels*, III, 70.

tinued to suffer for lack of adequate roads. Moreover, its promise of prosperity went unfulfilled: thirty years later the permanent population still numbered only seventy-five or eighty families. French Canadians for the most part, they were unenterprising and failed to use their commercial opportunities, while near-by St. Louis commanded the commerce of the valley. The habitants of Kaskaskia were not envious. They preferred the easier tasks of trapping and raising cattle, horses, swine, and poultry.

Pike was not happy in Illinois—less so, indeed, than in Indiana. Soon after his arrival he contracted measles, and the long illness so weakened his body that for several weeks he was unable to perform his duties. Letters to his family reflect his mental attitude.

"Clara has been considerably indisposed since last month with the fever," Pike wrote to his mother on September 8, 1803, "but she is now somewhat better. But the little girl [Clarissa] keeps her health which is extraordinary, as she sucks her Mama, when she has fever, and is cutting teeth at the same time. But the good weather is commencing and I hope it will restore us to our previous vigour."

This is the first reference to Pike's children. Several years later he wrote a relative that he had been the father of five children, but that all had died except Clarissa.

In a subsequent letter, dated February 6, 1803, the Lieutenant commented again on his wife's condition. To his young sister Maria, he wrote: "Clara is low in spirits and should cheer up and try to be lively—and laugh at half the world's folly and dispise the envy of the ballance." Again, during the same year, he remarked: "Clara is at present very nervous and her situation here is very lonesome as the ladies are by no means sociable—except old Mrs. Edgar. The river between us and

39

the hill on which we are situated are such serious obstacles to ladies as to render intercourse a little difficult."

Near the end of autumn in 1803 the Pikes were in better spirit. Clara had recovered her health, and the Lieutenant's letters reflected a more cheerful outlook. These worries were no sooner ended, however, than new ones arose. The infant daughter, Clarissa, developed a serious throat infection, and for several weeks her parents feared she would not live.

Little is known of Pike's activities at Kaskaskia from 1803 to 1805. Sometimes he journeyed to Cincinnati or Pittsburgh to obtain supplies, but most of his work was confined to routine duties of the post. He served briefly as adjutant for the troops in the Illinois country, and, according to his own statement some years later, was also for a short while commander of the post at Kaskaskia.

Meriwether Lewis, who had been at Wilkinsonville with Pike for a few months in 1801, was also at Kaskaskia in 1803. His mission there was primarily to recruit men for the first government expedition into the Louisiana Purchase, which he was to lead. As a matter of fact, Jefferson had selected him for this task even before negotiations had been concluded for the purchase of the vast region west of the Mississippi.

Within a few months after Lieutenant Lewis left Kaskaskia, Lieutenant Pike was also ordered to St. Louis, there to make ready for an expedition of his own to find the source of the Mississippi. Pike's years of self-discipline and his long experience, both as a barge commander on the Ohio and as an officer on the frontier, were now to have important use. He was physically and spiritually ready for the rigorous ordeals which lay ahead.

5

"A Barren Sand"

LIEUTENANT PIKE grew up and earned his fame in a
unique period of American history. It was an era of
fantastic diplomacy, treasonable plots, and sinister intrigues—the troubled beginnings of a great nation. It was a
time when the country was rich in vast but unexplored resources. It was the age of Aaron Burr and James Wilkinson,
of Thomas Jefferson and the Louisiana Purchase.

By 1800 the frontier of the United States already extended
to the Mississippi. Beyond that river lay the Louisiana country, which now possessed a peculiar interest for the young
nation. Spain had controlled this region from 1763 until 1800
and had watched with mounting anxiety the advance of American pioneers and filibusters in the trans-Appalachian West.
Sooner or later, the Spaniards reasoned, they would have to
face the problem of keeping Anglo-Americans out of this vast
and empty province. They must accept an eventual war or else
stop the settlement of the Old Southwest.

This could be done by two or three devices. For instance,
the pioneers had no outlet for their produce except by the
Mississippi, and Spain controlled its mouth. By denying them
the "right of deposit" at New Orleans, she could stifle western
trade. But the pioneers kept on coming. Spanish officials then

sent their agents into United States territory hoping to make life unbearable for the westerners: Indians were aroused, property seized, and atrocities committed against Anglo-American settlers.

Spain recognized the weakness of the government under the Articles of Confederation and knew that the country was powerless either to retaliate or to defend its own. Could not the western parts be separated and perhaps annexed to the Spanish empire? Spain's agents worked toward this objective.

One of these agents was James Wilkinson, who had been a brigadier general in the Continental Army. Wilkinson was one of the most egotistical, bombastic, treacherous, and inefficient personages in United States history—a set of characteristics which distinguished him as an early American villain. At times he could be genial and charming, but more often he was pompous, petty, and vindictive.

Theodore Roosevelt gave an apt description of Wilkinson in his *Winning of the West:* "He was a good-looking, plausible, energetic man, gifted with a taste for adventure, with much proficiency in low intrigue, and with a certain address in influencing and managing bodies of men. He also spoke and wrote well, according to the rather florid canons of the day. In character he can only be compared with Benedict Arnold, though he entirely lacked Arnold's ability and brilliant courage. He had no conscience and no scruples; and he had not the slightest idea of the meaning of the word honor; he betrayed his trust from the basest motives, and he was too inefficient to make his betrayal effective. He was treacherous to the Union while it was being formed and after it was formed."[1] Whatever his shortcomings, and they were many, he was a friend of Zebulon Montgomery Pike. Had there been no Wilkinson

[1] III, 143.

to send Pike on exploratory missions, Pike would be scarcely remembered today, either for good or for bad.

Born of good family on a plantation in Maryland, Wilkinson had enjoyed every advantage. By the time he was eighteen he had completed the study of medicine and was practicing in a small Maryland village. He joined the Continental Army in 1775, and although his military record was not distinguished, the tall, raw-boned youth nevertheless attained the rank of brigadier general while yet in his early twenties.

After a brief employment in Philadelphia, Wilkinson moved to Kentucky in 1783 and went into business there. Within a few years he had acquired a small fortune, built an expensive house in Lexington, and married into a prominent Philadelphia family. The Wilkinsons lived well and entertained expensively.

In July of 1787, Wilkinson made his first visit to New Orleans, hoping to "do business" with the distrustful Spaniards. He bribed his way into the acquaintance of the right people, one of whom was the governor, Esteban Rodríguez Miró. To Miró, Wilkinson whispered that the western settlements were discontented, that there was talk of secession, and that the revolt might involve an attack on Spanish Louisiana and Florida.

He lost no time in convincing Miró that Spain should renew her provocative activities in the Old Southwest. He even suggested that a local revolt might enable Spain to annex Kentucky and Tennessee. For Spanish gold and the privilege of trading at New Orleans, Wilkinson agreed to persuade certain westerners to seek the benefit of Spanish rule.

Returning to Kentucky, he now took full advantage of the commercial opportunities he had acquired at New Orleans. His barges of tobacco, flour, calico, and whiskey went down the

43

Mississippi without molestation from the Spaniards. With each shipment, Wilkinson sent dispatches to Miró proclaiming the conversion of Kentuckians to an ultimate alliance with Spain. For a time he fared well financially. His profits were enormous, his Spanish pension was adequate,[2] and he enjoyed a growing influence in Kentucky politics.

Yet, by 1790, Wilkinson was almost destitute. He had spent too freely and feasted too long while some of his ventures had been ill considered. In need of more income, he turned to the rejuvenated American Army.

He had perhaps never forgotten the sense of power his old uniform had given him, and longed to display it again among fine ladies and envious gentlemen. On November 7, 1791, President Washington appointed him, at his own request, "Lieutenant Colonel Commandant." Within a short time he had risen to the rank of brigadier general, then to major general. Before long he outranked all other officers and had command of the entire army.

He was in a position now to convince the Spaniards that his services were more valuable than before; and for several years he continued to deceive these gullible officials, telling them lies or giving them information of doubtful value. As his ruse continued to work, he played his double role for all it was worth.

Changing events, however, brought an end to Spain's need for his services. In 1792, Kentucky entered the Union as a state. Three years later, following the United States' treaty with England, from whom Spain had much to fear, the latter

---

[2] By 1796, Wilkinson had received approximately $26,000 in bribes from the Spaniards. For more complete data on his activities as a Spanish spy, see James Ripley Jacobs, *The Tarnished Warrior*, and R. O. Shreve, *The Finished Scoundrel.*

country hastened to negotiate with the United States, granting it the right of deposit at New Orleans. In 1796, Tennessee was admitted to the Union, and talk of western secession further diminished.

Then, on October 1, 1800, Spain secretly ceded the whole of Louisiana to France. Now, with such a barrier between her provinces and the United States, she hoped to be free from the threat of American penetration. Wilkinson's services, in consequence, were no longer needed, and his pension was discontinued.

Thomas Jefferson, the new president, was alarmed at the prospect of having France for a neighbor in the Southwest. He feared that the right of deposit would now be permanently denied and that political disorders would follow. Therefore he sent James Monroe to Paris to try to obtain assurances from Napoleon on the use of New Orleans or some other port on the Gulf of Mexico.

In the acquisition of Louisiana, Napoleon had had an ulterior purpose: he had long dreamed of a new French colonial empire in America with Louisiana as a base. But the transfer of the vast region had scarcely been accomplished before his grandiose scheme was thwarted by political changes in Europe. The old adage, "Europe's distress is America's advantage," was never more true than in 1803. The United States now purchased the entire Louisiana Territory, with the same area it had covered under Spain, for fifteen million dollars. On April 30, 1803, the treaty of cession was signed, and once again the Americans and the Spaniards were neighbors in the Southwest.

The purchase of Louisiana was easily Jefferson's greatest achievement, although he pretended that "it is a barren sand, which individuals will not buy; we gain nothing but peace." Actually, Jefferson had been interested in the vast region beyond the Mississippi for many years and before any thought was given to acquiring it.

On December 4, 1783, while in France, Jefferson had written to George Rogers Clark suggesting an overland journey from the Mississippi to the Pacific as a means of forestalling British rivalry. "I find that they subscribed a very large sum of money in England," he remarked, "for exploring the country from Mississippi to California. They pretend it is only to promote knowledge. I am afraid they have thoughts of colonizing into that quarter. Some of us have been talking here in a feeble way of making an attempt to search that country. But I doubt whether we have enough of that kind of spirit to raise the money. How would you like to lead such a party? Too, I am afraid our prospect is not worth asking the question."[3]

Two years later, in Paris, Jefferson talked with John Ledyard[4] about the latter's plan to cross Siberia to Kamchatka, then sail across the Pacific, and finally make an overland trip through Louisiana. This plan failed when Ledyard was turned back by Russian officials. In 1790, Captain John Armstrong made an attempt to explore the region, starting from the Eastern states, but he was stopped by Indians. André Michaux, the French botanist, started west in 1793. Upon Jefferson's recommendation, he was backed by the American Philosophical Society. Michaux, however, soon became embroiled in other matters and did not travel beyond the Mississippi.

When Jefferson became president in 1801, he again turned his attention to Louisiana. Even before the purchase of the

[3] From the *Original Journals of the Lewis and Clark Expedition*, edited by Reuben Gold Thwaites, VII, 193.

[4] John Ledyard as a corporal in the United States Marines accompanied Cook on his last voyage (1776–79) and later wrote *Journal of Captain Cook's Last Voyage on the Pacific Ocean*.

territory, as has been noted, he had asked Congress for permission to explore the region and had chosen Meriwether Lewis and William Clark to lead the expedition. This proved to be the first of several government-sponsored journeys into Louisiana.

Although exploration of the newly purchased territory was one of Jefferson's immediate concerns, the government of the vast province also demanded his attention. As a temporary expedient, he appointed two commissioners to govern Louisiana until Congress could enact appropriate legislation. They were W. C. C. Claiborne, the young and unimpressive governor of Mississippi Territory, and General James Wilkinson, commander of the United States Army.

Wilkinson's return to New Orleans in 1803 presented an opportunity to renew his former Spanish contacts. Spain was not happy about the transfer of Louisiana to the United States. Aware of this, the crafty Wilkinson obtained $12,000 from Spanish officials in exchange for "confidential information" (which they were unable to use) regarding military plans in the Southwest. At the same time, he dispatched to Washington data on Spanish forces and plans in the Southwest. He proved highly proficient at playing both ends against the middle.

In March, 1804, Congress created the Territory of Orleans from that part of the Purchase lying south of thirty-three degrees. The rest was to be organized into a Louisiana Territory, sometimes called Upper Louisiana. Claiborne was appointed governor of Orleans, while Wilkinson hoped to obtain the governorship of Louisiana. With this object in mind, he sailed for Washington early that summer.

The tarnished General's quest for the post had two motives, both financial. An additional stipend of $2,000 a year would allow him to gratify his expensive tastes, and as governor he would be able to "milk" the Spaniards of yet more money.

To obtain this appointment, Wilkinson now planned his campaign as carefully as a general going into battle. He remembered that even if the appointment were made by the President, it would have to be confirmed by the Senate. The president of the Senate was Aaron Burr, still an influential politician despite his waning prestige as a statesman.[5]

Burr and Wilkinson had known each other since the Revolution. They had never been jointly concerned in any great enterprises, although they had met and corresponded on several occasions since the war. In 1799, Wilkinson had visited Burr in New York, and in 1800, Burr had got the General's son into Princeton.

Down to the present day, Aaron Burr's character has remained an enigma. With a distinguished ancestry, he, like Wilkinson, had had all the advantages of a great family name. He was brilliant, well educated, handsome, and now in the prime of life. Also like Wilkinson, he was vain and ambitious. His record during the Revolution had been commendable. Since the war he had moved only in the higher circles of society and politics. In 1800, he had been elected vice-president of the United States and had tried to seize the presidency by a political trick, but had been thwarted in this attempt by Alexander Hamilton.

Before his term as vice-president expired in March, 1805, Burr sought the governorship of New York only to find that Hamilton again blocked his plans, despite the support of influ-

[5] Burr and Wilkinson served together creditably in the Battle of Saratoga during the American Revolution. By a strange twist of fate, another of their fellow officers in that engagement was Benedict Arnold. These three men rank today as America's foremost traitors.

GENERAL JAMES WILKINSON
from the C. W. Peale portrait

ential Federalists. When he returned to Washington during the summer of 1804, his political career had never appeared more uncertain, and he looked forward with apprehension to presiding over the "lame-duck" Senate.

On May 23, 1804, Burr received a message from James Wilkinson. "To save time of which I need much and have little," Wilkinson wrote, "I propose to take a bed with you this night, if it may be done without observation or intrusion. . . . Answer me and if in the affirmative, I will be with you at 30 after the 8th hour."[6]

The desire for secrecy on Wilkinson's part is obvious. He wanted no one to know that he proposed to talk with an avowed enemy of the administration. Jefferson had never forgiven Burr for his attempt to seize the presidency in 1800.

What the two men talked about on that May night remains clouded by rumor and suspicion. Few surpassed Burr in knowledge of politics in the East, while no one had traveled more widely in or possessed more information about the West than Wilkinson. Burr had previously talked of a new career in the West, and Wilkinson was seeking the governorship of Louisiana. In the light of subsequent events, it seems apparent, therefore, that they formulated a plan for their joint advantage.

General Wilkinson was the first of the two to get what he wanted. He received his appointment, although he did not take up his new post for several months. Meanwhile, Burr and Hamilton fought a duel, in which Hamilton was killed and as a result of which Burr's political fortunes were ruined. The former Vice-President now turned his full attention to plans for "liberating" the Spanish provinces in the Southwest, and perhaps separating the Western states from the Union. What

[6] For the full text of Wilkinson's letter to Burr, see Jacobs, *The Tarnished Warrior*, 211.

his plot actually contemplated is not clear even today, for all his stories were conflicting. Yet there is little doubt that his plan was a sinister one and that Wilkinson was involved in it.

Soon after his term of office expired, Burr left Washington for Philadelphia where he approached the British Minister, Anthony Merry.

". . . Mr. Burr has mentioned to me," Merry wrote to Lord Harrowby on March 29, 1805, "that the inhabitants of Louisiana seemed determined to render themselves independent of the United States and that the execution of their designs is only delayed by the difficulty of obtaining previously an assurance of protection and assistance from some foreign power and of concerting and connecting their independence with that of the inhabitants of the western parts of the United States, who must always have a command over them by the rivers which communicate with the Mississippi. . . ."[7]

Burr did not divulge the whole of his plans for the Southwest, but Merry had a vivid imagination. He knew that many Englishmen would be glad to see the Union dissolved, and he assured Burr of his personal favor. With high hope of British gold and military aid, the wretched opportunist set out on a tour of the West, eager to inspect his future domain while awaiting a reply from London.

Late in April, Burr was at Pittsburgh with his daughter, Theodosia, and a small party of western politicians, awaiting the arrival of General Wilkinson. But as the General was delayed, the Burr party sailed without him in a specially fitted boat, the *Ark*.

Taking leave of the other members of his party at Cincinnati in mid-May, Burr and his daughter journeyed over-

[7] See Walter F. McCaleb, *The Aaron Burr Conspiracy*, 25–26, for the full text of Merry's letter.

land to Lexington, Kentucky, where they were entertained by Henry Clay, and thence to Nashville for a visit with Andrew Jackson. The future President welcomed the former Vice-President with typical western hospitality. Jackson was impressed by the fine manners of his guests, and when they were ready to leave, he provided a boat and crew. Burr and Theodosia traveled down the Cumberland to the Ohio, where they met the *Ark.*

From the mouth of the Cumberland to Fort Massac on the Ohio was only a short distance. It will be recalled that old Major Pike had served as commandant here a few years earlier. When Burr reached Fort Massac in June, he found General Wilkinson awaiting him, and for four days the partners remained in secret conference. What they talked about can only be surmised. McCaleb, in his *Aaron Burr Conspiracy,* says that "no doubt the whole situation was canvassed; the probability of war with Spain; the ease with which Florida might be overrun; the matter of equipping an army which would sail from Vera Cruz to light the torch of insurrection in Mexico."

Their talks concluded, the two "friends" departed, Burr continuing to New Orleans and Wilkinson to St. Louis. Wilkinson had given Burr letters of introduction to influential men in New Orleans and had provided a barge and ten privates to transport him down the river. He reached New Orleans by June 25, 1805.

At St. Louis, the capital of Louisiana Territory, Wilkinson, meantime, busied himself with his duties and mentally reviewed his arrangements with Burr. It is hard to reconstruct his plans, for Wilkinson, like Burr, talked too much and told the truth too little.

Within less than a month after Burr's visit, Wilkinson

ordered an expedition to the source of the Mississippi. How long he had entertained the idea no one knows. Neither can anyone be sure that this venture had anything to do with the Burr conspiracy.

Isaac J. Cox argues that Wilkinson's action reveals already a decision to betray Burr's plan for his own particular interest.[8] He holds the opinion that Wilkinson's correspondence, together with his known relationship with the infamous Philip Nolan, justifies the assertion that the Mississippi-voyage in 1805–1806 formed a part of the General's private schemes.

As will be seen later, Wilkinson also authorized the Arkansas Expedition led by Pike, and the evidence against him in this instance is more persuasive. Undoubtedly, the Arkansas expedition did fit into Wilkinson's plans and possibly into those of Aaron Burr. But about the ulterior motives of these movements, more will be said later.

The Lewis and Clark Expedition to the Pacific Coast got off on May 14, 1804. Doubtless this venture gave Wilkinson the idea, or excuse, for a similar expedition to the source of the Mississippi. He knew that Jefferson desired all the knowledge available about Louisiana. It was also important to determine the northern limits of the Purchase. As commander-in-chief of the western army and governor of Louisiana Territory, Wilkinson had the authority to send out an exploring party into the region he governed.

On June 24, 1805, he wrote to Lieutenant Pike, then commander of the post at Kaskaskia, ordering him to prepare to embark from St. Louis, with all convenient speed, in order to explore the Mississippi to its northernmost source. Pike was to collect information on the number, character, and power of the Indian tribes. He was to offset the Spanish, French, and

[8] Isaac J. Cox, *The Early Exploration of Louisiana*, 105–16.

52

English influences among them, to collect scientific and astronomical data, to ascertain the geographic boundaries of Upper
Louisiana, to observe the soil and natural produce of the region, to determine the courses and navigability of the rivers,
and to choose sites for military posts and factories.

Pike eagerly embraced this opportunity for fame. He realized that the successful completion of his Mississippi voyage
would mean promotion and subsequent opportunities. Eager
to please his commanding general and to gratify his own desire
for action, he lost no time in preparing for the voyage.

Wilkinson may have had disloyal motives in sending Pike
into the Northwest. But the fact that he authorized the expedition without the President's knowledge does not necessarily
prove that he did. Communication was slow between the Far
West and the East. It would have taken at least two months
to exchange letters between Washington and St. Louis in 1805.
And by that time, the season would have been too advanced,
for it was Wilkinson's intention that Pike return to St. Louis
before the winter set in.

Jefferson was informed of the Mississippi expedition after
it left St. Louis on August 9, 1805. That he approved of Wilkinson's action is evident from his annual message of December 2, 1806, when he reported to Congress the results of the
Lewis and Clark Expedition and of Freeman's attempt to find
the source of the Red River. "Very useful additions have also
been made to our knowledge of the Mississippi," Jefferson
continued, "by Lieutenant Pike, who has ascended to its source
and whose journal will be shortly made ready for communication to both Houses of Congress."[9]

[9] James D. Richardson (ed.), *Messages and Papers of the Presidents, 1789–
1897*, I, 408.

53

6

"A Last Adieu"

IT was no easy task to outfit such an expedition in the brief
time allowed to Pike. First, he had to find quarters for his
family. Then a party of some twenty soldiers had to be
selected for the journey; they had to be young, strong, coura-
geous, and obedient. And last, there was the matter of equipment, food, and supplies.

We are uncertain whether Wilkinson had discussed the
voyage with Pike prior to his letter of July 24, 1805. Probably
the General had visited Lieutenant Pike at Kaskaskia before
going on to St. Louis from Fort Massac. But, at the most, Pike
had but little time for preparation—a fact that was to be only
too apparent later.

Pike reached St. Louis late in July, 1805. With him were
his family and about a dozen soldiers brought from Kaskaskia.
Quarters for his wife and daughter were found at Fort Bellefontaine, near St. Louis, and he then turned to selecting the
other members of his party from the troops at Bellefontaine.
They brought the number of the group to seventeen privates,
two corporals, and a sergeant.

Supplies and equipment for a four months' journey were
obtained at St. Louis. "I am at present at a very considerable
expence in fitting out Lieut. Pike, for I believe, the headwaters

of the Mississippi, and repairing two large boats stiled Stod-
dards and Lewises," wrote the assistant military agent at St.
Louis to the military agent at Philadelphia, on July 19.[1]

There is no record of the amount and kind of supplies
which Pike obtained; but judging from his diary, he carried
several small barrels of flour, whiskey, corn meal, pork, gun-
powder, salt, and tobacco. Quantities of calico and knives were
taken as presents for the Indians. Lead, writing paper, ink,
flags, hunting dogs, tents, clothing, blankets, and sundry provisions were also included. Equipment for the entire expedition seems to have cost the government about $2,000.

Only the crudest scientific apparatus was procured. Lieutenant Pike obtained a watch, a thermometer, and a simple in-
strument for determining latitude. He later complained that
all three were poor in quality and inaccurate; but they were
the best to be had at that time and place.

Oddly enough, no surgeon was appointed, although several army doctors were available, and one would be sorely
needed. Even worse, Pike was allotted no interpreter and so
was often to be at a loss in dealing with Indian chiefs. Likewise, another lieutenant of subaltern grade might have re-
lieved Pike of some of his duties and responsibilities.

Pike raised no objection to the personnel or outfitting of
his group, and his diary and letters reveal no doubt in his
mind concerning the adequacy of his previous experience. He
looked forward with confidence, reasoning that he would
rather trust his own resources than share command and honors
with another. Doubt of his ability was not like the man, and
if it had been, he would never have reached his objective in
the face of the many hardships he was to encounter.

[1] Clarence Mulford to William Linnard, July 19, 1805 (typed copy), Missouri Historical Society, St. Louis.

General Wilkinson's first written instructions to Pike were given him on July 24; a week later, on July 30, 1805, the General ordered him to proceed up river with all possible diligence: "You will please to take the course of the river and calculate distances by time," Wilkinson directed, "noting rivers, creeks, highlands, prairies, islands, rapids, shoals, mines, quarries, timber, water, soil, Indian villages and settlements, in a diary to comprehend reflections on the winds and weathers.

"It is interesting to the government to be informed of the population and residence of the several Indian nations, of the quantity and species of skins and furs they barter per annum, and their relative price of goods, of the tracts of country on which they generally make their haunts, and the people with whom they trade.

"You will be pleased to examine strictly for an intermediate point, between this place and the Prairies des Chiens, suitable for a military post, and also on the Ouisconsing [Wisconsin River], for a similar establishment; and will obtain the consent of the Indians for their erection, informing them that they are intended to increase their trade and ameliorate their condition.

"You will proceed to ascend the main branch of the river until you reach the source of it, or the season may forbid your further progress without endangering your return before the waters are frozen up.

"You will endeavor to ascertain the latitude of the most remarkable places in your route, with the extent of navigation and the direction of the different rivers which fall into the Mississippi, and you will not fail to procure specimens of whatever you may find curious, in the mineral, vegetables, or animal kingdoms, to be rendered at this place.

"Your own good sense will regulate the consumption of your provisions, and direct the distribution of the trifling presents which you may carry with you, particularly your flags.

"In addition to the preceding orders, you will be pleased to obtain permission from the Indians who claim the ground, for the erection of military posts and trading-houses at the mouth of the river St. Pierre, the falls of St. Anthony, and every other critical point which may fall under your observations; these permissions to be granted in formal conferences, regularly recorded, and the ground marked off."[2]

Although in this second letter Wilkinson made only a passing reference to the fur trade of the Northwest, some historians have believed that this was his principal concern in authorizing the expedition. Contrary to previous agreement, the British still maintained their trading posts south of the Great Lakes. British traders influenced the Indian tribes of the Northwest and realized handsome profits from their trade.

Wilkinson no doubt was confident that he could gain something for personal as well as for official ends from the projected Mississippi voyage. He had already arranged for goods from a Baltimore merchant, and these were to be shipped to St. Louis, moreover, in army barges, without charge for freight. It was neither the first nor the last time that he was to use his public office for private gain. Yet, in the end, Wilkinson must have reaped little personal benefit from Pike's voyage, for in 1806 he lost his governorship at St. Louis and was transferred to the South.

The personal interests of General Wilkinson were doubtless far from the Lieutenant's mind as he and twenty companions embarked at Bellefontaine in their seventy-foot keel-

[2] Original letter now in the War Records Division, National Archives, Washington, D. C.

boat on August 9, 1805. A journal kept by Pike, then twenty-six years of age, is the chief source of our knowledge about this expedition.[3]

Although it leaves much to be desired, this diary contains a day-to-day account of distances traveled, temperatures, Indians, fur traders, latitudes, and hardships encountered. It contains little in the way of description of the country and scanty details of probably dramatic happenings. Doubtless because he had no idea of publishing his diary, Pike noted only what he was ordered to record. Little effort was made, even later, to polish the manuscript or to give it more readable form.

In 1805, the upper Mississippi was remarkable for its great width and its hundreds of small islands. Sometimes the river seemed to lose itself in innumerable channels among these islets; sometimes the distance from bank to bank was five or six miles; and much of the surrounding land was flooded in rainy seasons. For several hundred miles above St. Louis the valley consisted of prairie and woodland; vines and underbrush grew thick in the forests, while in spring and summer the prairies were carpeted with flowers.

Pike and his companions found good sailing during the first few days of their journey. Their keelboat had a large, square sail, and with the aid of favorable winds and oars manned by the soldiers, it could travel sometimes as far as forty miles in the space of ten hours.

But the entire voyage was not to be so agreeable. Torrential rains ruined supplies and dampened the spirits of the men. Many delays were occasioned by the frequent channels, where it was only too easy to go astray. Because the stream was

[3] Pike's Mississippi journal was published in Philadelphia in 1810, along with the one kept on the Arkansas expedition in 1806–1807. It was subsequently republished in England, France, Holland, and Germany. All quotations from Pike's journal herein given are taken from the English edition (London, 1811).

THE EXPEDITIONS OF
Zebulon M. Pike

.... *Expedition to find the source of the Mississippi
River, 1805-1806*
----- *Expedition to the headwaters of the Arkansas
River, including travels in Spanish territory,
1806-1807*
.... *Route of Lieutenant Wilkinson to the mouth
of the Arkansas River, 1806-1807*

sometimes low, sand bars, stumps, and logs were a constant hazard and several times damaged the boat. For this portion of the journey, at least, an experienced guide would have saved the men much time and labor.

A few days above St. Louis, the explorers began to meet canoes of Indians; they were armed and could be formidable. But the whites were armed, too, and the red men usually kept their distance, believing the whites to be quarrelsome and dangerous. This was a favorable circumstance, and to maintain it, Pike assumed a cold and pompous attitude except when ashore and in council with the Indians.

On August 20, his party reached the foot of De Moyen Rapids (near present Keokuk, Iowa), a formidable obstacle which no one of Pike's men had previously crossed. According to the Lieutenant himself, the rapids were eleven miles long, with successive ridges and shoals from shore to shore. The river here was about three quarters of a mile wide, its banks grown up with cottonwood, ash, and hackberry.

Upon ascending the rapids about five miles, Pike's party encountered an Indian agent, William Ewing, and with him several Sac Indians, who had come to help the white men through the rapids. After several of the heavy supply barrels had been transferred to Indian canoes, the remainder of the rapids were negotiated without difficulty.

Above them was a Sac village, near present-day Montrose, Iowa, where Ewing had his headquarters. Here, after a stay of several days, Pike addressed for the first time an assemblage of local chiefs. The speech he made then he was to repeat frequently in the course of his journey.

"I spoke to them of the following purpose," Pike recorded in his diary on August 21, "That their Great Father, the President of the United States, wishing to be more intimately acquainted with the situation of the different nations of the red people in our newly acquired Territory of Louisiana, had ordered the General [Wilkinson] to send a number of his young warriors in different directions, to take them by the hand, and make such inquiries as might afford the satisfaction required." Impressed by his rhetoric and manner, the chiefs seem to have expressed only happiness at becoming the new children of a "Great White Father."

At daybreak Pike and his little crew embarked again. Despite an increasingly rapid current, the next few days afforded smooth sailing. Sometimes navigation was obstructed by the winding stream and the sand bars, but the beauty of the country was impressive. Trees were now more numerous, and signs of autumn were everywhere apparent.

Small bands of Indians were also seen more frequently. On one occasion, four men and two women were encountered on shore and, in the hope of obtaining fresh venison, Pike gave them a quart of whiskey diluted with water. This was eagerly accepted, but the red men pretended not to understand the request for venison. In disgust, the Americans returned to midstream, but soon heard shouts ashore and, looking back, saw the Indians holding up two hams of deer meat, dancing and shouting in childish glee.

On August 27, the voyagers passed the mouth of the Rock River, near present Davenport, Iowa. Here they met James Aird, a Scot trader employed by the Michilimackinac Company.[4] Aird, a genial character, was taking four loaded canoes downstream to trade with the Indians. Although Pike's rela-

[4] The Michilimackinac Company maintained its headquarters on Lake Michigan in 1805. It was second in size only to the Northwest Company, and had a capital stock of $800,000 at the time.

tions with Aird were most cordial, he was convinced that the
government should put a stop to British trade in the Northwest. Foreign traders brought in goods without paying any
tariff and were not always honest with their customers. Moreover, they had great influence with the Indians, and used it
often to the disadvantage of the United States.

After questioning Aird about the course of the stream
above and cautioning him about his illicit trade, Pike went on
his way. Just above the mouth of the Rock, the party found yet
swifter rapids, but with the greatest of luck got the keelboat
safely past them. It was a chilly business, however, for with
the approach of September the weather was getting colder.

Fortunately, the winds continued favorable, and the boat
made good time. At noon on September 1, it reached what is
now Dubuque, Iowa, the site of Julien Dubuque's lead mine.
In keeping with his instructions from Wilkinson, Pike questioned the operator about the extent of his production.

Dubuque had had a mining concession from the Sioux Indians and, after the purchase of Louisiana by the United States,
had obtained permission to go on with his work. An industrious
man, he seems to have mined from 20,000 to 40,000 pounds
of ore a year. The ore was approximately 75 per cent pure
lead and was now making the owner rich. Wilkinson very
probably wanted to take advantage of this venture, but it was
not for Pike to question the motives of a superior. With solemn
honesty, he carefully inspected the Dubuque mine and sent
a full report to the General at St. Louis.

Before Pike's arrival at the mine, two of his party had got
lost while hunting for some dogs that had strayed out of camp.
Pike now waited for them for several days, but when the men
did not appear, fearing they were dead, he at last determined
to go on without them.

Meanwhile, the lost soldiers had indeed nearly perished, having wandered six days with no food but mussels. Aird, the Scot trader, eventually found and fed them and took them to a near-by Fox village, where they were kindly received. The Fox chief gave them corn and clothing, and put them in a canoe manned by two braves, and they reached Pike's camp just before he re-embarked. Great rejoicing followed.

Prairie du Chien, a former French settlement above the mouth of the Wisconsin, was reached on September 4. Pike estimated its population at around five or six hundred whites. It was the largest settlement he had encountered and for many years had been the center of a thriving fur trade. Pike found its stores and houses well built, comfortable, and spacious.[5]

Prairie du Chien lay in the midst of a small and beautiful prairie, about a mile from the Mississippi and four miles above the mouth of the Wisconsin. Behind it were several high, bald hills; much of the surrounding land was marshy, and the climate seemed unhealthy. With its mongrel population and unrestricted sale of liquor, the town had gained a reputation for violence and murder, but apparently the French and Indians had lived in some degree of harmony, for half the inhabitants were of mixed blood.

It occurred to Pike that here would be an excellent site for a military post. So he remained for several days to explore the country and to hold a council with the Winnebago chiefs. To them he again made his imposing speech, telling them of their new status under the United States government. At its conclusion athletic contests were held between the Indians, villagers, and soldiers. Pike records that his men beat all the

[5] Visitors to Prairie du Chien fifteen or twenty years later described the settlement as being in a state of decay.

others in running, jumping, and hopping, gaining the respect-
ful awe of the red men.

As he prepared to leave, it became apparent that his way
would now be harder, for above him the river was obstructed
by falls and rocks. Abandoning the large keelboat, he procured
two smaller boats, and hired a half-blood named Rousseau as
interpreter and guide.

Two days above Prairie du Chien the party arrived at the
first Sioux village on the Mississippi. It seemed peaceful
enough, but inshore the voyagers were greeted by a hail of
shot. They backed water with a rush, only to realize that this
was in fact a welcome. News of Pike's approach had preceded
him upstream. The Sioux warriors had prepared to receive
him in style, but some, unhappily, had got drunk in the process.
Their enthusiasm having now the upper hand, they began firing over the heads of the men and into the water, their shots
too close for comfort. As he stepped ashore, Pike carefully
held one hand on his pistol and the other on his sword.

Leaving his troops to guard their boats, Pike accompanied
Chief Wabasha to his lodge. There the two, with their interpreter, sat on clean mats and pillows to smoke the pipe of
peace. When Pike explained the nature of his visit, Wabasha
replied that he had never been at war with his new Father
and hoped he never would be. He was not a warrior, he said,
and he knew the Indian could not live without his white
brother. He meant to remain at peace.[6]

After their talk, Pike and Wabasha had a meal of wild rice
and venison, and food was sent also to the soldiers at the boats.
After dinner the white men witnessed a dance by the warriors

---

[6] Wabasha was one of the few Sioux chiefs who did not go to war with the
United States in 1812. Major Stephen Long, who visited the old chief in 1823,
called him "Wapasha."

and Indian women. "They were all dressed in the gayest manner," Pike recorded; "each had in his hand a small skin of some description, and would frequently run up, point their skin, and give a puff with their breath; when the person blown at, whether man or woman, would fall, and appear to be almost lifeless, or in great agony; but would recover slowly, rise, and join the dance. This they called their great medicine . . . the Indians believing that they actually puffed something into each others' bodies which occasioned the falling."

Before taking leave of Chief Wabasha next morning, Pike gave him several gifts—knives, calico, salt, tobacco, and watered whiskey. The expedition then pushed off in the face of a cold north wind, for winter was fast approaching.

Along the banks were now many bald hills, their lower slopes covered with birch, elm, and cottonwood. A continuous succession of high perpendicular cliff and low valleys, matted with cedar, traversed the country at right angles to the river. "But this irregular scenery," Pike later wrote, "is sometimes interrupted by a wide extended plain which brings to mind the verdant lawn of civilized life, and would almost induce the traveler to imagine himself in the center of a highly cultivated plantation."

A few miles above the Sioux village the travelers noticed several fresh mounds of dirt on a distant prairie. Thinking them Indian graves, Pike halted to investigate and found them to be breastworks lately erected by the Sioux. Some were half-moon shaped and others round, while the earth had been scooped out to form what we now call "fox holes." When attacked by an enemy, the Sioux would immediately dig in with their knives, tomahawks, or wooden spades and then crawl into the holes, where they were safe. The Indians in this area, unwilling to pay the price in casualties, would never storm fortified positions. Pike later found that the Chippewa to the north practiced a similar defense.

Lake Pepin, as the French called it, the next landmark of the journey, was just a wide place in the Mississippi, bordered by jagged cliffs. It was about one and one-half to four miles in breadth, and some twenty-two miles in length. Rousseau, the interpreter and guide, declared the lake unsafe for their small craft in daylight because of high winds, and, although it was now evening, insisted that they cross before morning. Reluctantly, Pike assented, although he felt the real motive was Rousseau's fear of the Chippewa. Indeed, the tribe was said to have ambushed several travelers where the Chippewa enters the Mississippi to form this lake.

"We sailed with our violens and other music playing," Pike records. The early part of the crossing was pleasant enough, but a sudden gale threatened their craft, and the party had to put in at a small bay on the east shore for the rest of the night.

As morning approached and a more violent storm appeared imminent, Pike determined to embark at once and complete the crossing before the worst arrived. Setting sail at half-past six, the voyagers were no sooner in the middle of the lake than heavy gales and torrential rain descended on them, forcing a landing at Point Sable.

On coming ashore, Pike found another stranded traveler, one Murdock Cameron, a Scot trader, comfortably encamped in a tent, his canoe unloaded and turned over his goods to protect them. Cameron proved an interesting storyteller, entertaining Pike for hours with legends of the country. Pointing out a distant cliff, called "Maiden's Rock," the Scotsman, thoroughly in key with the romanticism of the period (and of several succeeding and preceding periods), told of an Indian girl who had leaped from it to her death rather than marry a man she did not love. "A wonderful display of sentiment in a savage," Pike thought at the time and later noted in his journal, himself as sympathetic as the narrator.

When the storm subsided, Pike routed out his troopers and crossed the lake without further incident, entering again the winding Mississippi. Four days later, on September 21, the party reached the mouth of the St. Peters River[7] and halted on the eastern shore to take their meal.

Here on the site of what is now St. Paul, Minnesota, was a Sioux village of eleven lodges. Pike found the river at this point so narrow that he could cross it by canoe with only forty strokes.[8] Finding none of the inhabitants in the village, he passed on when the meal was finished.

From the mouth of the St. Peters River (St. Paul) to the Falls of St. Anthony (Minneapolis), the Mississippi was one continuous narrow rapid or fall, its bottom rocky and its channel narrow. High hills covered with maple, ash, and cedar rose from the banks, while clear blue water flowed from many springs, tumbling over the rocks and cliffs. Wild geese and duck were everywhere.

Suddenly Pike observed a white flag on shore and, upon investigation, found it to be a piece of white silk hung over a scaffold. Beneath were the fresh bodies of three Sioux women and a child, wrapped in blankets and covered with bark. Pike subsequently learned that two of the women had been wives of Frenchmen, and that all four Indians had died of natural causes. Bodies of Sioux who had died by violence would have been left uncared for.

[7] By act of Congress, June 18, 1852, the St. Peters was renamed after the state of Minnesota, through which it flows.

[8] Major Long in 1813 crossed at this same spot, from a dead start, in sixteen strokes.

That night the party encamped on what is now called Pike Island, a few miles below present Minneapolis. Remaining there for several days, Pike busily explored the land on both banks for a distance of several miles. On September 23, at a council with the Sioux chiefs and their warriors, he signed a treaty purchasing 100,000 acres lying on either side of the river.[9]

". . . the Sioux nation grant unto the United States, for the purpose of establishment of military post," the treaty read, "nine miles square at the mouth of St. Croix, also from below the confluence of the Mississippi and St. Peters [Minnesota] up the Mississippi to include the falls of St. Anthony, extending nine miles on each side of the river, that the Sioux nation grants to the United States the full sovereignty and power over said district for ever. . . .

"The United States promise, on their part, to permit the Sioux to pass and repass, hunt, to make other use of the said districts as they have formerly done without any other exception than those specified."[10]

The Sioux also got trade goods, then and there, to the value of about two hundred dollars.

This treaty was the principal achievement of Pike's voyage. Here in 1820 was built Fort St. Anthony, later Fort Snelling, for many years an important military post. The Lieutenant, elated with his bargain, wrote to General Wilkinson that the tract was worth $200,000.

Wilkinson, however, seems not to have shared his subordinate's enthusiasm and to have thought the price too high,

[9] This tract included most of the present area of the twin cities, St. Paul and Minneapolis.

[10] The original treaty is now in the War Records Division, National Archives.

for he wrote the Secretary of War, on November 26, 1805, that Pike was "a much better soldier than negotiator." Nevertheless, army officers who inspected the tract in later years called it the "finest site on the Mississippi for the construction of a fort," a tribute to Pike's judgment.

Having composed what he called "a last adieu to the civilized world," Pike sent letters to his wife and General Wilkinson by special carriers, and then embraced the task of getting upriver to the head of the Falls of St. Anthony. So swift was the current that the boats had to be carried all the way overland. Pike expressed disappointment in the falls for their beauty was not what the Indians and traders had led him to expect. Today they are little more than ripples, but in 1805 they were still boisterous, tumbling cataracts, and few white men had gone beyond them.

Above the Falls of St. Anthony, the river was sometimes deep and narrow; the land was flatter and more prairie-like; scrub oak dotted the landscape, and elk, bear, deer, beaver, buffalo, raccoons, and fowl were much in evidence. Occasional falls were encountered, while a continuous chain of islands lay ahead as far as the eye could see.

Sometimes the men had to wade for hours, pushing and pulling their boats through the swift current. Frequent rains augmented their discomfort, and by early October the temperature at night would fall to zero. Their only compensation was the variety of meat they now enjoyed.

Supplying the party with wild game was largely the task of two members of the group, Bradley and Sparks. They usually remained ashore and kept up with the canoes, hunting and sometimes spying out the land ahead. Frequently Pike himself walked with the hunters, for none was a better shot. He had good need to be: each man consumed seven or eight pounds

69

of meat daily, and a supply had to be laid in for the winter when game would be scarce.

Frequent delays were occasioned by the need for curing this meat. Usually it was "pickled" in salt, sometimes broiled or smoked. The soldiers' favorite dish consisted of meat, either fresh or cured, boiled in a pot with flour, wild rice, or corn so as to make a thick soup. Sometimes each man cooked his own meal, but when such a soup was prepared, it was made all in one big pot. If meat was scarce, a man would get only two pounds a day, usually with an extra gill of whiskey for consolation. When meat was plentiful, however, three full meals were enjoyed by all.

Generally they broke camp about six o'clock in the morning and traveled for perhaps two hours before halting for breakfast. Dinner would be after one o'clock, and supper around six in the evening. At night huge fires were built, and before bedtime, there would be talk, cards, or the music of violins. Guards were posted, the soldiers taking turn in alternate watches of two hours each.

Against the biting cold, the men wrapped themselves in woolen blankets and lay as close to the fire as they dared. At each changing of the guard, fresh logs were added to the blaze. Pike almost always slept inside one of the tents erected to protect his supplies from rain or snow. Each night before retiring, he brought his charts and observations up to date and made an entry in his journal. Sometimes the ink froze in the bottle, and he often found himself too cold to sleep.

By mid-October snow had begun to fall, and boat travel became increasingly difficult. Pike, now aware that he could not this season reach the source of the river, hoped at least to push on to Crow Wing River before making permanent camp. This was the highest point yet reached by traders in their bark canoes, and the journey was now a race against time to achieve it. Yet even this modest goal soon appeared too much for the men.

"My Sergeant Kennerman," wrote Pike on October 16, "one of the stoutest men I ever knew, broke a blood-vessel and vomited nearly two quarts of blood. One of my corporals, Bradley, also evacuated nearly a pint of blood when he attempted to void his urine. These unhappy circumstances, in addition to the inability of four other men, whom we were obliged to leave on shore, convinced me that if I had no regard for my own health and constitution, I should have some for those poor fellows, who were killing themselves to obey my orders."

Pike therefore reluctantly decided that the next likely spot must be his winter camp. This proved to be in the vicinity of Swan River, near what is now Little Falls, Minnesota. Here Pike gave orders to halt and construct a stockade, for the game was plentiful, the country beautiful, and there were at hand abundant trees for huts and pine canoes. By the Lieutenant's own estimate, he was now over 233 miles above the Falls of St. Anthony and 1,500 miles from St. Louis.

From October 16 to 28, most of the party were employed in erecting the stockade, which was to be thirty-six feet square, with one blockhouse on the northwest corner and another on the southeast. Others were put to felling trees and building canoes, while Pike and his two hunters went out in search of game.

Pike planned to leave a small detachment at the stockade, while he and the others pressed on to the source of the river. But much had to be done before this final lap of the journey could begin. He spent one full day writing letters and making arrangements in the event he should not return. To Sergeant

Kennerman, who was to command the stockade in his absence, Pike gave rather explicit orders, which the man later disobeyed both in general and in particular.[11]

On October 28, the new pine canoes were finished and laden; but on their launching, one of them sank, badly damaging a quantity of ammunition and baggage and causing a delay of several weeks. Another canoe had to be constructed while Lieutenant Pike tried to salvage his powder by drying it over a fire in pots, one of which exploded in the process. The supply of ammunition was now so reduced that the party could not have survived a prolonged Indian attack.

Work on the canoes progressed slowly. For the first time Pike complained of his condition, writing that he was "powerfully attacked with the fantastics of the brain called ennui." He could now readily understand why men confined in remote places got to drinking, and how others fell on bad habits just to pass the time.

To distract his mind, he spent many hours a day rereading the few books he had brought along. He also went hunting and did whatever work lay at hand. Now that there was time, Pike had the stockade enclosed with pickets as a further precaution against attack. "Had it not been for political reasons," he wrote, "I would have laughed at the attack of 800 or 1000 savages, if all of my party were within."

On December 10, after the canoe and some sleds had been finished and a quantity of venison provided for each party, Lieutenant Pike with eleven soldiers and the interpreter Rousseau, departed from the stockade. Their destination was Lake Leech, then thought to be the source of the Mississippi River.

[11] Sergeant Kennerman later accompanied Pike on his Arkansas expedition in 1806–1807, only to desert after the first few weeks. His behavior on both expeditions is discussed in subsequent chapters.

7

"Never . . . More Fatigue"

IT was on December 10, six weeks after Pike first prepared to leave his stockade that he finally began the last leg of his journey. Meanwhile, as the river had partly frozen and was now impossible of ascent by canoe, he had had to have two large sleds constructed to haul his supplies. Each sled was drawn by two soldiers geared abreast, while six others were employed to drag the two canoes. Two barrels of provisions, totaling four hundred pounds, were loaded on each sled; while part of the baggage and lighter equipment went in the canoes.

Above the stockade at Swan River the environs of the Mississippi were prairie, with occasional groves of pine. Snow mottled the ground, and for a time it was with great difficulty that Pike's eleven made so much as five miles daily.

Four days out, an unfortunate accident nearly ended the expedition, for, being moved too near the river, one of the sleds upset and broke through the ice. Although his men jumped waist deep into the icy water to salvage equipment, all of Pike's baggage and books, a supply of cartridges, and four pounds of double-battle Sussex powder were sadly damaged.

Indeed, when they halted to build a fire and dry out the supplies, it was found that the cartridges and choice powder were a complete loss; most of the common glazed powder, tightly corked in kegs, was undamaged. The sled itself, broken beyond repair, had to be replaced before the party could move again. Meanwhile Pike went hunting and in the course of three days got eleven deer and one buffalo.

To make room for this fresh meat, he had to leave part of his supplies behind. On the night of December 17, he dug a large hole, four feet deep, three feet wide, and six feet long, to hold a barrel of flour and one of pork, all wrapped in seven deerskins to resist the dampness of the earth. After filling in the hole with dirt, the men built a fire so as to make it look like a camp site and deceive the Indians. This cache, as it was called, was near present Fort Ripley, Minnesota; and another was made in the same manner an additional few days' journey.

Each day the wind grew colder and traveling more hazardous. Usually Pike walked in advance of the sleds, exploring the country, building fires for the soldiers, selecting camp sites, and occasionally going back to help his men. "Never did I undergo more fatigue," he wrote, "performing the duties of hunter, spy, guide, commanding officer . . . sometimes in front, sometimes in the rear and frequently in advance of my party 10 or 15 miles. At night I was scarcely able to make my notes intelligible."

When the river had frozen solid, the canoes were loaded on the provision sleds; and with three or four men to a sled, the party began to move up midstream. Although the ice occasioned frequent falls, travel was now much faster than across the rocky ground.

On December 23, they reached the mouth of Crow Wing River, and two days later had pushed on to the present Brainerd, Minnesota. On Christmas Day each man got two extra pounds of meat and flour, a gill of whiskey, and some tobacco. Above Brainerd the land was a dreary and barren prospect of rocks and snow, dead timber, and frozen lakes.

Signs of Indians were observed soon after Christmas, and the first Chippewa were met on January 2, 1806. On that day, just as the men were retiring a sentinel anxiously warned that a small party of Indians were approaching full speed. Hasty preparations for a fight proved needless, however, for it was soon apparent that the savages were on a friendly visit.

The party was composed of four Chippewa and an Englishman and a Frenchman, the two latter being employees of the Northwest Fur Company. From the Indians, Pike learned that they had discovered his camp some days before and had believed his party to be a band of warring Sioux. Their joy at finding them Americans on a peaceful mission was unconcealed, and Pike, to return their friendly gestures, now gave them half a deer. The Englishman, Cuthbert Grant, spent the night. He had several trading posts in this region, and early next morning he invited Pike to visit his headquarters on Cedar Lake (then called Lower Red Cedar), a few miles northeast of present Brainerd.

The course of the Mississippi here may be compared in shape to a buttonhook. Going upstream from the site of Brainerd, it curves to the right in a huge arc. About eighteen miles above Brainerd, on the right bank, is Cedar Lake, and about thirty miles farther on is the somewhat larger Sandy Lake, where Grant maintained a second trading post.

Farther up, the course of the narrowing river veers to the north and then turns off northwest, the radius of this arc being about forty miles. At the top of the arc, some seventy miles due north of Brainerd, the main course of the river passes through Lake Winnibigoshish. It can be followed west to Lake Cass, on to Lake Bemidji, and thence southwest to Lake Itasca, the ultimate source of the Mississippi.

Pike visited all of these lakes but the last two, and also Lake Leech, a few miles south of Lakes Winnibigoshish and Cass. This body of water connects with Winnibigoshish and Cass by a narrow channel and with the Mississippi by another stream flowing eastward toward what is now Grand Rapids. It was on attaining Lake Leech that Pike thought he had reached the principal source of the Mississippi, an error which will be discussed further later in this volume.

At Cedar Lake, Pike and one of his corporals had gone with Grant, leaving the men to continue the march upriver. At first sight of Grant's house, Pike observed a British ensign flying from the roof. Somewhat embarrassed, Grant hastened to explain that it belonged to some Indians and had not been displayed by him at all. Pike accepted the explanation without comment, and the three men sat down to a hearty breakfast.

After finishing his meal, Pike received several Chippewa chiefs and promised to return in a few days and hold a council with them. He and the corporal then went back to the river and caught up with their sleds before the end of the day.

On the night of January 4, Pike was suddenly aroused from his sleep by the cry of one of his sentinels, "God damn your souls, will you let the Lieutenant be burned to death?" His first impulse was to seize his gun but discovered that some of his tents were on fire. The blaze was extinguished only after extensive damage had been done.

Several tents were a total loss, not to mention Pike's socks, which had been hung up to dry, his leggings, moccasins, and most of his bedding. Fortunately, three small casks of powder had been saved. Without them, the expedition would have been helpless to ward off attack and unable to kill game for food. This proved to be the last of three serious accidents, any one of which might have decided the fate of the expedition, if not indeed cost the lives of the men.

In the first week of January, "some of the men had their noses, others their fingers, and others their toes frozen." Scouts went ahead of the main party to build fires every two or three miles, and traveling became extremely slow. On January 6, Pike and one soldier, wearing snowshoes, pushed on ahead toward Sandy Lake (then called Lac de Sable), which they reached on January 8. Here Grant maintained another trading post and, having arrived a few days before, again received guests with his accustomed hospitality.

It was not until January 13 that the rest of Pike's party arrived, and here for the first time in months they had the luxury of warm and comfortable quarters. Yet, although the agent was a generous host, Pike felt it necessary to "attend Grant's motives with careful observation."

The few white traders of this northern country lived better than he had anticipated, even though obliged to content themselves with Indian women. "They have horses, raise plenty of Irish potatoes, catch pike, suckers, pickerel, and white fish in abundance."

The Indians gathered wild oats, or rice, in the swamps and sold it at the trading post for $1.50 a bushel. The agents sold the Indians flour at fifty cents a pound; salt at one dollar a pound; pork at eighty cents; and sugar at fifty cents. All the provisions except the sugar, which was made from the sap of native maple trees, were imported from England or Canada. Even so, the Northwest Company's profits often exceeded 1,000 per cent.

Pike found the Chippewa around Sandy Lake less warlike than he had been led to expect. They held the Americans in greater veneration than they did any other people, saying that they were neither French nor English, but "white Indians." Nevertheless, British traders still exerted an enormous local influence, and during the War of 1812 most of the Chippewa tribes fought against the United States.

Within a few days Pike began to prepare for the journey to Lake Leech, then commonly believed to be the chief source of the Mississippi. This last lap of the journey would be the most difficult, and Pike began by constructing lighter sleds, more practical than those hitherto employed.

These new sleds were each of one large plank, turned up in front like a fiddlehead, and to them was lashed the baggage, packed in duffel bags. Having employed a Chippewa for a guide, Pike planned to depart on January 20, only to find then that the sleds were too heavily laden. Much of the baggage and food had to be left at the Sandy Lake stockade.[1] In the rush Pike left behind his salt and ink, a loss greatly regretted later.

With his guide and Private Boley, he now moved on ahead of the sleds and followed the course of the narrowing Mississippi as it twisted its way toward the northwest. The Chippewa deserted en route. Late in the afternoon of January 26, Pike and Boley reached the site of Grand Rapids, where Grant had a third trading post. Two days later, when the other men had arrived with their sleds, Pike renewed the journey upriver, again traveling in advance, now accompanied by Corporal Miller.

---

[1] These supplies were never recovered, for the expedition returned by a different route; but they were badly needed before the Americans reached St. Louis.

This part of Minnesota was dotted with hundreds of lakes and swamps all rimmed with patches of oak, pine, cyprus, and maple trees. The few trails were covered with ice and snow, and the bitter cold was scarcely bearable. In the late afternoon of January 30, about thirteen miles northwest of the Grand Rapids post, Pike and Miller came on a Chippewa lodge.

Here an Indian lived with his wife, five children, and an old woman. "They received us with every mark that distinguished their barbarity such as setting their dogs on ours, trying to thrust their hands into our pockets. . . . But we let them know that we were not afraid, and let them know we were Chewockomen (Americans) when they used us more civilly."

After establishing his camp near by, Pike entered the lodge in hope of obtaining food. In exchange for a small plate of dried beef, he gave the man and woman two gills of whiskey. They then offered more meat, to get another round, and on the Lieutenant's refusal, offered beaver skins, but still to no avail.

A similar episode occurred next morning, when Pike gave the Indian another dram of whiskey before asking directions to Lake Leech. "It really appeared that with one quart of Whiskey, I might have bought all he possessed," wrote Pike.

From the Indian lodge, Pike and Miller now followed the Mississippi to its fork a few miles distant. One fork continued northwesterly to Lake Winnibigoshish and thence through Lake Cass to Lake Itasca, the real source of the river; while the other passed through a meadow from the west. Pike chose the latter course, thinking it would lead to Lake Leech.

Most of the meadow was swampland with occasional ridges of pine, elm, ash, oak, and maple. Arriving on the shores of Lake Leech around two in the afternoon on February 1, Pike supposed he had at last reached his objective. "I will not attempt to describe my feeling on the accomplishment of my voyage, for this is the main source of the Mississippi," he exclaimed in his journal.

Lake Leech is about thirty miles due west of Grand Rapids and connects with the Mississippi by that small stream, flowing east, which Pike had lately traveled. During the wet seasons, this stream could supply the Mississippi with more water than any of its other northern tributaries; but it is often dried up in the summer.

From Lake Winnibigoshish, the route upriver continues through Lakes Cass and Bemidji, and then turns south to Lake Itasca near the present Clearwater.[2] Although Pike recognized Lake Itasca as one source of the Mississippi, he failed to visit it, and so missed by some twenty-five miles the ultimate source of the "Father of Waters."

Soon after arriving at Lake Leech, Pike and Miller looked up the Northwest Company headquarters on the lake shore. Its proprietor, Hugh McGillis, received them with typical frontier hospitality, offering the unwonted luxury of hot coffee, butter, and cheese.

Not until six days later did the main body of Pike's men reach the headquarters, affording the Lieutenant time for a well-earned rest. His host, moreover, had a good library, and Pike read eagerly when not in council with the Indians or conversing with McGillis.

Despite the geniality of his host, Pike could not approve of all his practices. As a matter of record, he addressed a letter to McGillis outlining his objections: the trader was not to fly

[2] Lake Itasca is approximately 2,555 miles from the Gulf of Mexico. It was first visited by an American in 1804, when William Morrison from Kaskaskia, Illinois, reached its shores. Morrison is discussed later in this book in connection with Pike's Arkansas expedition.

Valley of the St. Peters, *c.* 1820

New Orleans, 1812
view taken from the plantation of Marigny

the British flag, or distribute flags, medals, and liquor to the Indians, or ignore the tariff payable on British goods.[3]

McGillis readily agreed to all these conditions. In a formal reply he even expressed an admiration for the Americans and their government, whose laws he claimed never to have violated in any case. This was hardly in keeping with the man's reputation, for he was reputed a sworn enemy of the United States and a notorious liquor trader, if not worse.

It must be conceded, however, that McGillis behaved very well to the Americans, giving them food and warm shelter, and going with them up to Lakes Cass and Winnibigoshish. He also sent one of his clerks all over the region to call the Indians into council, and later gave the Lieutenant two sled dogs worth two hundred dollars.

Seemingly, Pike did not return McGillis' kindness, except to mention in his diary that the trader had been helpful. Perhaps he was justified in view of the suspicion touching British traders in general. In the presence of McGillis and several Chippewa, Pike had his men and the Indians shoot down the Union Jack and hoist the United States flag in its place.[4]

On February 12, Pike and one soldier, with McGillis and two of his men, went up to Lake Cass, spent the night at the northernmost point attained on the journey (latitude 47° 42′ 40° N, according to the Lieutenant's calculations). "This may be called the upper source of the Mississippi," he remarked in his journal, "being 15 miles above Little Lake Winipie [Lake Winnibigoshish] and the extent of canoe navi-

[3] Pike estimated the loss in taxes to the federal government at $26,000 annually.

[4] During the War of 1812, McGillis was very effective in enlisting the help of the Chippewa against the Americans.

gation only two leagues to some of the Hudson's Bay waters." It was the only one of the upper Mississippi lakes that Pike visited.

On his return to the trading post, February 14, he found several Chippewa, chiefs and warriors, awaiting him. At a council two days later Pike again explained the nature of his visit and told the Chippewa they were now all children of a "Great Father" in Washington. It was moreover the "Great Father's" desire that his Chippewa make peace with their ancient enemy, the Sioux. And Pike asked that several of their chiefs go with him back to St. Louis for a council with General Wilkinson.

Each chief now arose in turn to express respect for his new "Father" and the desire of northern tribes to have peace with those to the south of them. Everyone was most agreeable, but no one could undertake the journey to St. Louis. Who could say but what the young bucks might make the war path in their absence?

Pike, chagrined at this refusal, for Wilkinson had specially desired to hold a council, feigned surprise to find their hearts so weak, saying that the tribes to the south would think them cowards. Two of the young braves, Buck and Beau, now volunteered to make the trip, and Pike, accepting them as his children, gave each a blanket, a pair of leggings, scissors, a looking glass, and a small dram of whiskey.[5]

His mission accomplished, Pike began the return journey on February 18. His men were now equipped with snowshoes and carried part of their supplies by dog sled. Again the Lieutenant, this time with his two Indians and one soldier, blazed a trail for the main party. He laid a new course overland toward the southeast in the hope of reaching Cedar Lake.

[5] Buck and Beau deserted on February 28.

Although few trees impeded travel, the frozen, rocky ground make walking as difficult as at any previous time. Five days' march brought Pike's advance party to the Mississippi near the place where they had camped on January 2. It was here that the Americans had first met Cuthbert Grant not far from his Northwest trading post on Cedar Lake.

Reaching Grant's house on February 25, Pike found himself now utterly exhausted. His feet, cut and bleeding from the racket strings on his snowshoes, had to be treated before he could go farther. On February 27, the rest of the party arrived, but they were not allowed to tarry long. Pike had decided against going to Sandy Lake to get the provisions left there and had determined to set out for his Swan River camp at once.

Consequently, on March 1, the expedition returned to the Mississippi and continued their southward march. Traveling lighter than in the past two months, and through a region they knew, the Americans now made rapid progress. Previous encampments were passed in quick succession, and the barrels of flour and meat which had been cached on December 17 and December 20 were recovered in good condition.

Crow Wing River, where two men from Pike's Swan River stockade were encamped, was reached by March 3; but the joy of reunion was dispelled by the sad news Pike received. Sergeant Kennerman, in charge of the stockade, had acted disgracefully, using up all of the hams and saddles of venison stored for the return voyage, and either drinking or selling the whiskey. He had squandered most of the flour, pork, corn, salt, tobacco, and Indian presents, and had even opened Pike's trunk and dispersed his personal effects. "How mortified the disappointment," recorded the Lieutenant.

On arrival at the stockade two days later, Pike found these

charges were indeed true. Only his previous fondness for Kennerman prevented his punishing the wretch as he deserved. Kennerman was merely reduced to a private. Had such an incident occurred on the Arkansas journey, a few months later, Pike would certainly have had the Sergeant shot. One learns to be hard on the frontier, or he does not live.[6]

Pike and his party remained at the stockade for more than a month before resuming their voyage to St. Louis. Because the river was frozen over, they had to wait until the ice broke before attempting to travel by canoe. Meanwhile, the untiring Pike further explored the region around Swan River. He reached the present Spunk River, with his interpreter, and arrived at the lodge of a Menominee chief on March 18.

Here an amusing incident occurred. The chief received his visitors in patriarchal style, giving them dry clothing and a warm supper. The Lieutenant got a soft bearskin for his bed, with a large feather pillow, and was then offered, for his greater comfort, one of the chief's wives.

"This," he observed, "in the eyes of the contracted moralists would be considered a monster of libertinism; but by a liberal mind would be considered as arising from the hearty generosity of the wild savage. In the course of the day, observing a ring on one of my fingers, he inquired if it were gold; he was told that it was a gift of one with whom I should be happy to be at this time; he seemed to think seriously and at night told my interpreter, 'That perhaps his father' (as they all called me) 'felt much grieved for the want of a woman; if so, he could furnish him with one.' He was answered that with us each man had but one wife, and that I considered it strictly my duty to remain faithful to her. This he thought

[6] In 1807, when one of his men complained of the heavy load he had to carry, Pike warned the man that more grumbling would cause his execution.

84

strange, he himself having three, and replied that 'He knew some Americans at his nation who had half a dozen wives during the winter.' The interpreter observed that they were men without character; but that all our great men had each one wife. The chief acquiesced, but said he liked better to have as many wives as he pleased."

Before the ice could break and free the river, Pike had another visit from the English trader Grant. With him were several Chippewa chiefs, some unknown to Pike, who had come downstream for a meeting with Pike and other Indians around Swan River. The Lieutenant had hoped to hold an amicable council with the Chippewa, Sioux, and Menominee, but as the Sioux would not come, the meeting was held without them.

On March 27 all the warriors crowded into Pike's stockade to hear speeches by their own chiefs and by the Lieutenant himself. Breche-dent, one of the Chippewa chiefs, concluded his talk by handing Pike a peace pipe, asking him to take it to the Sioux and have them smoke it. Attached to the pipe were seven strings of wampum, which, the chief explained, denoted seven bands of Chippewa, who were willing either to conclude peace or to declare war, at the wishes of the Sioux.

Pike now supplied his guests with liquor, so that each could drink to the health of all. But it was with a sigh of relief that he saw the Indians depart the next morning, for in three days they had consumed almost his whole supply of meat.

It was more than a week after the conclusion of this council before the river was open to navigation. Meanwhile, canoes had been made ready, supplies packed, and the date of departure set for April 7. "All hearts and hands were employed in preparing for our departure," Pike recorded. "In the evening [April 6] the men cleared out their room, danced to the violin, and sang songs until eleven o'clock, so rejoiced was every heart at leaving this savage wilderness."

Their boats were loaded and ready by ten o'clock the next morning. Of course, the return voyage would take far less time than the northward journey several months before. (In fact, the trip from Swan River to St. Louis required but slightly over three weeks, compared to an upstream journey of two months.)

The last lap of the voyage was bare of incident save for a brief stop at Prairie du Chien on April 18. Here Pike held a second council with Wabasha, chief of the Sioux. Also present were several chiefs and warriors of the Fox and Winnebago tribes. Wabasha received the pipe sent by Breche-dent, and all the Indians smoked it, in token of perpetual peace with the Chippewa. The Lieutenant, gratified at the time, was soon to learn that maintaining peace among the tribes was not wholly a matter of peace pipes.

After the conference the Americans were entertained with a ball game between the Indian tribes. From Pike's detailed description, it appears that the game was like a combination of modern soccer and hockey. The contest, with the Sioux on one side and the Fox and Winnebago on the other, was played on a near-by prairie, both sides laying heavy bets before the game began.

Playing with a small, hard ball covered with leather, the contestants numbered nearly three hundred braves. Each carried an object resembling a butterfly net on the end of a three-foot stick; or perhaps it more nearly approximated a long-handled tennis racket with the strings quite loose to catch the ball. The object was to put the ball between the opponent's goal posts, and the two goals, incidentally, were nearly half a mile apart, allowing plenty of room for the contestants. In point of casualties, the contest more nearly resembled a battle than a ball game.

It lasted for several hours and was not concluded until one side had made four goals. Sometimes the ball was knocked along the ground, but more often it was passed from player to player. Apparently, the rules were very simple, a player being able to run with the ball, kick it, knock it, or pass it to a teammate. It required considerable skill and endurance, and often the ball would not touch the ground for an hour or two, except when put in play after each goal was scored. Because of their superior skill in throwing the ball, the Sioux won the game, although Pike found the Fox and Winnebago much swifter of foot.

Not until three days later did the Americans resume their homeward journey. A few hours after embarking, Pike met a barge from St. Louis carrying a letter from his wife, the first word from her since his departure in the previous August.

On April 30, 1806, the party arrived at St. Louis, ending a journey begun almost nine months before and covering a distance of more than five thousand miles.

The accomplishments of Pike's Mississippi voyage, in the words of one western historian, were "disappointingly meager."[7] Here is the record in relation to his principal objectives.

Pike had been ordered to ascend the Mississippi to its source, to investigate the fur traders and stop their illicit trade, and to make peace among the Indian tribes. That he failed to reach the true source of the river is a fact of but slight importance. His menacing gestures toward the Northwest Company were unavailing, for British traders continued to ignore the United States tariff. Nearly all the Indians he visited joined

[7] See Robert E. Riegel, *America Moves West,* 138.

the British in 1812. And soon after Pike's return the Sioux and Chippewa renewed their habitual war.

Although Wilkinson had instructed Pike to bring back several warriors from each of the northern tribes for a council at St. Louis, the Lieutenant had been unable to get a single one to accompany him.

Yet, cheerfully ignoring these apparent failures, Pike supposed he had achieved a permanent peace among the Indians. Never one to underestimate his own accomplishments, he recorded in his journal on March 13, "If a subaltern with but 20 men, at so great a distance from the seat of his government, could effect so important a change in the minds of those savages, what might not a great and independent power effect, if, instead of blowing up the flames of discord, they exerted their influence in the sacred cause of peace?"

As for scientific and geographical information acquired, it was negligible. Pike located not a single stream or lake not previously discovered and named. The maps he made are poorly drawn and very inaccurate, while his journal is full of errors and contradictions, badly arranged, and very difficult to follow.

There is something to be said in Pike's favor, however. His diary, when published in 1810, awakened considerable interest in the Upper Mississippi Valley. Valuable tracts had been acquired, one of which became the site of Fort Snelling, a very important western post. Moreover, as a result of Pike's reports, illicit British trade in the Northwest was eventually stopped.

Probably his most important contribution was to focus attention on the disputed boundary dividing the Louisiana Purchase from Canada. In 1805 the British were claiming the territory as far south as the Missouri. Thirteen years later the present boundary was laid out from the Great Lakes to the Rockies. Undoubtedly the United States would not have had so good a claim to Minnesota had not Pike explored it in 1805–1806.

Although Pike would be little remembered today solely on the record of his Mississippi voyage, it was this expedition which fitted him for the greater tasks of 1806–1807.

8

"Many Things Improper to Letter"

PIKE returned to St. Louis confident that his exploits had earned him a needed rest and an immediate promotion, but he was to be disappointed in both assumptions. His captaincy was not to come until August 12, when he was in the West; and his vacation did not materialize at all.

For although Wilkinson was pleased with his protégé, he felt obliged to assign him at once another and similar task. Pike was now ordered to explore the upper waters of the Arkansas and the southwestern portions of the Louisiana Purchase. Moreover, the new expedition had to start as soon as possible, for time apparently was all important to Wilkinson's current scheme.

In the weeks following his return from the upper Mississippi, Pike labored busily preparing his journal and reports, whose composition betray his haste and carelessness. Mrs. Pike, meanwhile, saw little of him, for no sooner did her husband complete his writings than he commenced great preparations for his journey to the Southwest.

Throughout 1805 and 1806, while Pike was mostly away exploring, James Wilkinson and Aaron Burr were sowing the

90

seeds of a plot which was to bear them evil fruit—indeed, to disgrace them both—and to render Pike himself suspect.

Burr had arrived in New Orleans in June, 1805, while Pike was fitting out his Mississippi expedition at St. Louis. Thanks to letters from Wilkinson, the former Vice-President was welcomed by prominent citizens, especially by one Daniel Clark. To him, Wilkinson had written, "If the persecutions of a great and honorable man can give title to generous attention, he [Burr] has claims on all your civilities and all your services. You can not oblige me more than by such conduct, and I pledge my life it will not be misapplied. To him I refer you for many things improper to letter, and which he will not say to any other."[1]

This last statement is typical Wilkinsonese. That he and Burr were up to something is evident, but what their play may have been is problematical. Burr, deliberately or otherwise, started many rumors in New Orleans, but perhaps only to cover up his real design.

We know that he consorted with members of the Mexican Association, a body of some three hundred Creoles, former Spanish and Mexican citizens, New Orleans merchants and adventurers, who for years had talked of liberating Mexico. Daniel Clark was a member and had long dreamed of a Mexican revolution. However, he was not at all interested in separating the Western states from the Union and, alarmed at current rumors, wrote to Wilkinson a few days after Burr's departure from the city.

"Many absurd wild reports are circulating here—respecting our ex-Vice President. You are spoken of as his right hand man. . . . The tale is a horrid one. . . . Kentucky, Tennessee, the State of Ohio, with part of Georgia and Carolina, are

[1] Shreve, *The Finished Scoundrel*, 140.

to be bribed with plunder of the Spanish countries west of us to separate from the Union."[2]

Burr had reached St. Louis before Clark's letter arrived, having gone over five hundred miles out of his way to visit Wilkinson a second time. What they talked about in that September of 1805, is matter for speculation. Wilkinson himself testified two years later that Burr had declared that the federal government was dying a natural death and the West was ripe for revolt.

The immediate effect of Clark's letter is likewise unknown. There is some evidence that by late summer Wilkinson no longer shared Burr's confidence in a western secession. The purchase of Louisiana in 1803 had of course resolved many local complaints, and, save for a few diehards, most westerners were now "strong for Jefferson and democracy." A man of Wilkinson's experience must have detected this change in public feeling. I. J. Cox believes that Wilkinson was now prepared to betray Burr, but there is little positive evidence.

Wilkinson's own story of his relations with Burr cannot be trusted because of the General's own dubious character. In 1807, when Burr was on trial for treason at Richmond, Wilkinson swore he had written to the Secretary of the Navy, just after Burr's return from New Orleans: "Burr is about something, but whether internal or external I cannot discover. I trust you should keep an eye on him." (No trace of this note could be found, but the General was "almost sure" he had written it.)

At the same time, Wilkinson produced a copy of a letter he claimed to have written to William Henry Harrison, then governor of Indiana Territory, but there is no evidence that

[2] See *ibid.*, 143, for full text of Clark's letter to Wilkinson, September 7, 1805.

the letter was delivered. In it the General suggested that Harrison get Burr elected territorial delegate to Congress, where "he would be rendered harmless." If the letter were actually sent, it may have been a deliberate deception to distract attention from the principal plot.

Late in 1805, Burr was again in Washington to raise money and solicit aid for his western enterprise. Evidently the English were not interested, for they had failed to reply to Merry's letter of several months before. Perhaps they feared that Burr's ambitions and their own would clash in the Spanish Floridas.

Burr now turned to the Spaniards themselves. One of his confederates approached Yrujo, the Spanish minister, offering to prevent the United States from seizing West Florida and New Mexico, and to procure secession of the Western states and the formation of a union friendly to Spain. Although Yrujo was cordial, the Spanish government proved unwilling to risk financial and military aid to Burr, for he was himself untrustworthy, and his western friends were known to hanker after booty.

With hope of foreign aid lost, Burr solicited private sources. Friends and acquaintances, lured by the promise of fabulous gain, eventually put up some $50,000, the chief contributors being Herman Blennerhasset and Burr's own son-in-law, Joseph Alston. Meanwhile, a number of young adventurers had been assembled, supplies had been purchased, and barges constructed, all in the summer and fall of 1806.

Apparently, Burr hoped to depart for the Southwest, starting from Blennerhasset's island in the Ohio, before the end of November. The success of his enterprise depended in part on a war with Spain, which seemed likely in the immediate future.

However, he had made other arrangements in case such a conflict should be delayed. While in New Orleans, he had contracted to buy a half-interest in the Bastrop lands near Natchitoches, Louisiana. Here he could await an opportunity to launch his attack, either on New Orleans or on Vera Cruz, and thence on Mexico City. The lands would serve for a "mere pretense," as Jefferson later phrased it, until the United States Army under Wilkinson engaged the Spaniards in New Mexico and Texas, or until events in Europe should render Spain defenseless. Burr could then march unopposed into Mexico, where wealth and power would be his for the taking.

When Louisiana was purchased in 1803, it had possessed no definite southwestern boundary: Jefferson had claimed to the Río Grande, but the Spanish authorities had held out for the Arroyo Hondo. Gradually the United States abated its claims and retreated to the Sabine River, west of the Arroyo Hondo, whereupon the land between, later the famous Neutral Ground, became for some years a bone of contention between the Spaniards and the Americans.

By 1805, Spain had garrisoned the frontier settlement of Nacogdoches, west of the Sabine, while American soldiers held Fort Claiborne, at Natchitoches, just east of the Arroyo Hondo. When Spanish troops now boldly moved up to the Arroyo Hondo, wild excitement swept the American public, who called upon their government to drive them out.

However, it was not until the spring of 1806 that Jefferson, ever slow to war, ordered the governors of Orleans and Mississippi territories to reinforce Fort Claiborne and transferred General Wilkinson from St. Louis to command the troops in the South and repel any invasion from Texas.

Here was the moment for which Burr and Wilkinson had planned—the long-expected brink of war with Spain. Only the timing was premature: the General had not heard from Burr in several months and knew not when to expect his arrival on the Mississippi. Furthermore, Wilkinson had just arranged to send Lieutenant Pike into the Southwest to spy out the land; and as Pike had not yet departed, he could not now return in time to aid the General's plans.

For two months, Wilkinson temporized. He ignored the President's order while speeding Pike on his way, telling him to write often en route to Santa Fé, and to return to Natchitoches via the Red River. Only then, although there was still no word from Burr, did the General finally depart on June 11 for lower Louisiana. "Unavoidable delay" was the only excuse he gave the Secretary of War for his neglect of the President's command.

Arriving at Natchez in September, Wilkinson dashed into action with the energy of a dozen men. All available regulars and militia were ordered to Natchitoches, whence, the General boasted, "the enemy would be pushed westward clear to California." Within two or three weeks an impressive force had gathered along the east bank of the Arroyo Hondo, and when Wilkinson moved them across to the disputed area and encamped, a clash seemed unavoidable.

Unavoidable, that is, had not Lieutenant Colonel Herrera withdrawn his forces across the Sabine and so robbed Wilkinson of his chance for sudden fame and honor. Chagrined but undaunted, the General now resolved to pursue the Spaniards at whatever cost in time and preparation. But on the evening before Wilkinson was to begin his offensive, an unforeseen event changed all his plans.

The almost forgotten letter from Burr, together with another from his fellow conspirator Jonathan Dayton, arrived at the General's camp on October 8, 1806, brought by a trusted

95

messenger. Both letters were in code, and Dayton's being the shorter, Wilkinson deciphered it first. "It is well ascertained that you are to be replaced at the next session [of Congress]. Jefferson will affect to yield reluctantly to public opinion, but yield he will. Prepare yourself therefore for it. . . . You know the rest."[3]

Burr's missive read in part:"Your letter, postmarked thirteenth May, is received. I, Aaron Burr, have obtained funds and have actually commenced the enterprise. Detachments from different points and under various pretenses, will rendezvous on the Ohio, first of November. Everything internal and external favors views. Naval protection of England is assured. Truxton is going to Jamaica to arrange with the admiral of that station. It will meet us at the Mississippi. England, a navy of the United States are ready to join, and final orders are given to my friends and followers. It will be a host of choice spirits. Wilkinson shall be second to Burr only; Wilkinson shall dictate the rank and promotion of his officers. Burr will proceed westward first August never to return. . . . Already are orders given to the contractor to forward provisions to points Wilkinson may name. . . . Burr's plan of operation is to move down rapidly from the Falls on the fifteenth of November, with the first five hundred or one thousand men, in light boats now constructing for that purpose; to be in Natchez between the fifth and fifteenth of December, there to meet you; there to determine whether it will be expedient in the first instance to seize on or pass by Baton Rouge."[4]

This was very disturbing to General Wilkinson in the light of his imminent dismissal; without a command, all schemes

[3] McCaleb, *op. cit.*, 68.

[4] For the full text of Burr's deciphered letter of July 29, 1806, see McCaleb, *op. cit.*, 68–69.

AARON BURR

for Mexico and the Southwest would have to be laid aside. Moreover, western newspapers had for several months been denouncing the General as plotting to revive the old Spanish Conspiracy and break up the Union. Wilkinson was not unmindful that some of these papers must have reached Washington; and he reflected that a summons to the capital at this time, to answer such charges, would be most embarrassing, if not indeed fatal to his career.

Within a remarkably short period, he now decided upon a bold course of action: he would quiet these ugly rumors and at the same time rescue his country, emerging himself her savior and her hero.

Ten days after the receipt of Burr's communication, Wilkinson dispatched a letter to the President. In a dramatic, even hysterical, manner, he informed Jefferson of a fearful plot to destroy the Union, one that "staggered belief and excited doubt." Fortunately the General had learned of the project in time—he would end his differences with the Spaniards and send all troops to the defense of New Orleans.

President Jefferson had for several weeks heard rumors of Burr's activities, but it had been supposed that he merely intended to seize public land somewhere in the West. The receipt of Wilkinson's message prompted Jefferson to call an emergency cabinet meeting. Wilkinson might not be worthy of much credence, but the public demand for action could no longer be ignored. At his cabinet's suggestion, Jefferson warned Americans by proclamation against joining any military expedition into Spanish provinces. The cabinet further declared its approval of Wilkinson's peace with the Spaniards and suggested that New Orleans be fortified.

Not long thereafter, Jefferson had a second letter from the General, now very busy saving his country. Wilkinson assured

97

the President that the western papers "bespattering me with obliquity" had been established by the Federalists to discredit the administration and insure its defeat in the next election. He had already instructed his attorney in Kentucky to bring suit for libel against "said" newspapers.[5]

Meanwhile, on the Sabine, Wilkinson had concluded an agreement with Lieutenant Colonel Herrera, of the Spanish Army, in October. Wilkinson was to retire to Natchitoches and remain east of the Arroyo Hondo, while the Spaniards were to withdraw behind the Sabine.[6] Although this was just what the Spaniards wanted, Wilkinson could make it appear to his soldiers and the inhabitants of Louisiana that the enemy had backed down after a show of force.

Jefferson approved this agreement, but failed to announce its terms. Much later, in the Adams-Onis treaty of 1819, the Sabine was taken for the southwestern limit of Louisiana, but the United States was obliged to pay hard cash for the Neutral Ground after Spain produced the hitherto unpublished Wilkinson-Herrera agreement.

General Wilkinson himself, having achieved "victory" without bloodshed, now hastened to New Orleans, arriving before the end of November. There he at once wrote to the feckless governor, W. C. C. Claiborne, declaring that "you are surrounded by dangers of which you dream not. . . . The storm will probably break in New Orleans where I shall meet it and triumph or perish."

Claiborne, frightened out of his wits, scrupled not to place

---

[5] No record of such suit has ever been uncovered. Nevertheless, Wilkinson's letter to Jefferson had the desired effect, for he was retained as commander of the army.

[6] For many years this Neutral Ground was a haven for outlaws from the United States and Mexico. It was rumored that many of Burr's men fled to this region after the arrest of their leader.

his fate in the hands of a former personal enemy. "The hero of the Sabine" continued to fan the flames of fear and hysteria, assuring the people of the city that, indeed, their very lives and property were in immediate danger. He read them parts of Burr's deciphered letter, adding or omitting portions to suit his purpose. He did not neglect to keep his "friends" in Washington supplied with all details. A continuous stream of letters from him flowed into the capital, declaring that the situation "grows more desperate by the hour," and that drastic measures were indicated—for instance, martial law and the suspension of habeas corpus. "I feel certain," he wrote to Jefferson, "that my actions will be vindicated."

For some reason, the President was slow to act on Wilkinson's charges against Burr. Indeed, McCaleb suggests that Jefferson had intended "to lie still and leave Mexico to the filibusters of the West as he left Venezuela to those of Miranda, but it was the cry of treason that aroused him." In view of Jefferson's usual briskness, McCaleb's theory bears the color of truth. Then, two months after receipt of Wilkinson's first warning, the President issued a proclamation for the arrest of Aaron Burr. Burr, however, had already departed for Louisiana, and the warrant did not overtake him until he reached Tennessee.

The story of his subsequent arrest and trial is history. Brought before the United States Circuit Court in Richmond on charges of treason, he was the principal in one of the most sensational trials in the history of the American bar. Chief Justice John Marshall, a Federalist, who presided, was pitted against his political enemy, Thomas Jefferson, who in turn was resolved upon Burr's conviction.

James Wilkinson, the protégé of Jefferson, was to be the star witness. His journey from New Orleans was a triumphal

99

procession marked by receptions and banquets, with lavish toasts in honor of the savior of his country, but the General's luck was finally to run out in that little courtroom. "I was more on trial than Burr," he later complained to Jefferson. And, as a matter of truth, the longer the court stayed in session, the more overwhelming became the evidence against Wilkinson.

Both of the principals in this exciting drama were legally acquitted of treason. However, Burr's career was finished and his reputation forever tarnished; today his name is a synonym for treachery. Wilkinson, although he was to remain in the army until 1815, never overcame the stigma of his former association with Burr. Few people, the administration perhaps excluded, believed him wholly guiltless. One notable exception was Zebulon Montgomery Pike, who remained all his life, and to his frequent embarrassment, a staunch friend and defender of the now discredited General.

Pike did not get back from his southwestern tour until the Burr trial had well begun. Meanwhile, he had been captured by the Spaniards in what is now Colorado, taken to Mexico, and there held prisoner for several months. His arrival at Natchitoches in July, 1807, was unfortunately timed, for he found himself at once under suspicion. Many called him a dupe of Wilkinson's and believed his late journey to be part and parcel of the affairs of Aaron Burr.

9

"You Will Be Held Responsible"

ON June 24, 1806, Lieutenant Pike received a letter from General Wilkinson detailing the objectives of the Arkansas expedition. Restoration of certain Osage captives to their homes on the Grand Osage River in what is now Missouri was to be the principal aim. These Indians, captured by the Potawatomi several months before, had been released to the military commander at St. Louis, and Wilkinson thus made provision for their return.

The expedition was to establish a lasting peace between the Kansas and Osage nations in Louisiana Territory and to reach some understanding with the Comanche. Pike was cautioned that the latter task might lead him to the head branches of the Arkansas and Red rivers, close to settled parts of New Mexico. "There it will be necessary that you should move with great circumspect, to keep clear of any hunting or reconnoitering parties from that province and to prevent alarm or offense."[1]

As usual, the Lieutenant was to observe the geography, natural history, and population of the country through which he passed. In addition, he was to collect and preserve mineral

[1] Wilkinson's original letter of instructions is now in the War Records Division, National Archives.

and botanical specimens, to regulate his course by the compass and calculate distances by the watch, to ascertain exactly the latitudes and the variations of the needle, and to observe the eclipses of Jupiter's satellites.

The expedition would proceed to the source of the Osage and thence to the Arkansas River, which part of the expedition would descend to Fort Adams on the Mississippi. The remaining explorers would meanwhile continue to the source of the Arkansas, turn south, and descend the Red River to Fort Claiborne at Natchitoches, Louisiana. Pike was to map the two great rivers carefully. Nor, seemingly, was this all.

"It is well understood that Pike had secret instructions from the traitor, General Wilkinson," says Elliot Coues in his edition of Pike's journals, "over and beyond those which were ostensible; and no doubt the main purpose of his expedition was to open the way to Santa Fe, with references to such military operations as then seemed probable."[2]

Not until three weeks after receipt of Wilkinson's letter did Pike's expedition get under way. Meanwhile, he had again moved his family to Fort Bellefontaine, fourteen miles above St. Louis, where they were to remain during most of his absence. And it was from this settlement that the expedition eventually embarked on July 15.

Eighteen of the men who had accompanied Pike on his previous journey were enlisted for the second one. In addition, Lieutenant James B. Wilkinson, son of the General, Dr. John H. Robinson, a volunteer surgeon, one interpreter, and two privates joined the party. Two large river boats were now employed, instead of the one which had been used in 1805 and which had proved so inadequate. A greater variety of food

[2] This belief held by Coues and others is discussed more fully in a later chapter.

and also a telescope were procured. Unfortunately, since Pike did not believe that he would encounter as much cold weather as in the North, very little winter clothing was provided. This error was soon to be regretted, for the climate of the Rocky Mountain region proved to be more severe than that of the Minnesota area.

Fifty-one Osage Indians accompanied the party, and a strange sight they must have presented as the cumbersome river crafts, with their motley crew of sweating men and passengers, of Indian children and old women, pushed slowly up the broad Missouri.

Near present Jefferson City they entered the Osage River. This stream was then clear and beautiful as it coiled its way among the cedar-covered bluffs and through the fertile slopes of the Midwest. As Pike and his party ascended it, they were constantly awed by the abundance of buffalo, elk, antelope, bear, and deer that roamed the grassy banks and virgin woodlands, furnishing an ever present and inexhaustible supply of meat. Cottonwood, ash, oak, pecan, hickory, and elm were thick in the rich bottom lands. Not for another generation would this primeval domain be marred by the white man's civilization.

Navigating western rivers proved to be a difficult task. Although each of the two boats was equipped originally with a square sail and mast, these were soon discarded. The soldiers were forced to row against the sluggish current until shallow water was encountered, when long poles were more effective than oars. Several men were then ranged on either side of a craft, each holding a pole grounded in the river bed. Leaning against their poles they would walk toward the stern, slowing forcing the boat against the current. Where the water was swift and shallow, the crew would leap overboard and push the boat ahead of them. Frequently tow ropes had to be employed, part of the men pulling from shore while others pushed from behind.

Most of the Osage trudged along the bank, while those unable to travel afoot, particularly women and children, rode in the boats. In this manner the party made ten to fifteen miles a day. Often Lieutenant Pike and his two hunters trekked along with the Indians to hunt or explore. At night the Osage camped apart from the whites, who slept near the river to guard their boats and supplies. The Indians, usually about a hundred yards away, preferred some point higher than the river bank.

"Every morning we were awakened by the mourning of the savage who commenced crying about daylight, and continued for the space of an hour." On inquiry Pike learned that this was a custom not only of those who had recently lost a relative, but also of those who recalled the loss of some friend, perhaps long dead, and joined the others out of sympathy. The mourners sobbed bitterly as they sang their songs of grief: "Our enemies have slain my father, he is lost to me and my family; I pray to you, Oh Master of Life! to preserve me until I avenge his death, and then do with me as thou pleaseth."

The crying always ceased as suddenly as it began, when the braves would dry their tears and go about their business. Breakfast finished and the boats reloaded, both parties struck camp and resumed their toilsome journey. From St. Louis to the Grand Osage village, near the Missouri-Kansas line, the country was a hunter's paradise and "one of the most beautiful the eye ever beheld." Pike predicted that some day these extensive prairies, now covered with grass and flowers, would be the seat of a profitable ranching industry.

For the first few weeks the expedition was dogged by constant rain. Several men were sick from exposure and were unable to help with the boats. As if this were not enough, Private Kennerman, who had behaved so badly on the previous trip, now disappeared, never to be heard from again.

On the other hand, deer, buffalo, turkey, geese, and fish were so plentiful that the members of the party were able constantly to gorge themselves with food; and this time Pike carried a bountiful supply of coffee, a luxury not provided for the earlier voyage.

To keep up morale and beguile their brief leisure, there were frequent shooting matches for the soldiers and warriors. Usually the Lieutenant himself won these contests, for he was an excellent marksman. The regular army muskets of 1806 were long flintlocks of the Charleville French type,[3] accurate up to about fifty or sixty yards. Each contestant would stand erect, holding the nine- or ten-pound musket off hand, the target set at approximately forty paces. A simple cross, a few inches square, was the usual target, and each marksman would endeavor to place his bullet squarely in its center. The winner always got a prize of some sort, and if Pike won, he would give his trophy to one of the others.

By mid-August, 1806, the first objective was achieved when the party reached Grand Osage[4] and delivered the In-

---

[3] These arms, model 1795 Springfields, were faithful copies of the famous "Charleville" muskets of France. They were .70 caliber, with a barrel forty-five inches long. Ordinarily, special frontier exploring parties were equipped with rifles instead of muskets. Whether Pike's entire party was so equipped is not certain, but he did carry his personal rifle on his Mississippi and Arkansas expeditions. See Philip B. Sharpe's *The Rifle in America* for a history of American firearms.

[4] At the time of Pike's visit, the Osage people were divided into two main groups, the Great Osage and the Little Osage. Their nation consisted of several villages, scattered a few miles apart. Grand Osage was the home of the principal

dian captives to their people. "The reunion," Pike remarked, "was such as to make a polished society blush, when compared with those savages, in whom the passions of mind, whether joy, grief, fear, anger, or revenge, have their full scope."

Apparently Pike had more time to write in his journal of the manner in which the Plains Indians lived than he had found in the case of the Indians of the Upper Mississippi Valley. Or perhaps he simply found them more interesting. In many respects these tribes did possess a higher culture. For one thing, although the Osage had an oligarchic government, laws proposed by their chiefs had to be ratified by the people. Most of the males were warriors, and the remainder, cooks and doctors. These medicine men influenced the councils of the nation by "their pretended divinity, interpretations of dreams, and magical performances." The cooks were either for public use or attached to the families of some great men, depending on the source of their support.[5] All agricultural labor was done by women, for it was beneath the dignity of the males.

Sweet corn boiled in buffalo grease, meat, and pumpkin made up their staple diet. Lieutenant Pike, however, was treated to a bowl of hot tea, served with a wooden spoon, and

chief of the Osage. Authorities differ as to its exact location, except that it was somewhere near the present boundary of Kansas and Missouri, perhaps not far from the site of Oswego, Kansas.

[5] The French traveler Victor Tixier visited among the Osage in 1840. His account of the "cooks" and their position in society differs somewhat from Pike's account: "In this nation there are poor people; and those who are poor have no horses, no means of hunting . . . in order to secure meat. They own neither huts or blankets; they live, so to speak, at the expense of the community. If one of these unfortunates comes to the hut of a warrior and says: 'I am coming to your lodge;' the brave replies: 'This is good!' The poor man becomes his guest; he eats, smokes, and warms himself at the fire of the warrior; he does as he likes without ever being asked to account for his actions; he will never be compelled to do any work and will be waited on."—*Tixier's Travels on the Osage Prairies* (edited by John Francis McDermott), 135.

one of boiled meat to be eaten with a horned spoon; for, according to Pike, his host on this occasion was a chief who had been to the States and had carefully observed the ways of the whites.[6]

Pike found the Osage village to consist of several lodges very close together and distributed in a circle. At night all horses and stock were driven into the enclosure to prevent theft. During the winter these lodges were abandoned for tepees in the woods.

Before he departed, Pike and his men were invited to a ceremonial dance in which the braves performed feats of skill and daring. One Osage warrior asked Pike what he would give to see him run a stick through his tongue and let someone cut off the end. On Pike's promise of a shirt, the Indian, apparently with great pain, forced a stick through his tongue. Thereupon a bystander pretended to cut off the tip of it, which was held up to public view before being rejoined to the rest of his tongue. Turning to the Lieutenant, the performer asked what he thought of the feat. "I replied," commented Pike, "I would give him twenty shirts if he would let me cut off the piece from his tongue. This disconcerted him a great deal, and I was sorry that I had made the observation."

On August 18, as Pike prepared to resume his journey, he received an express from General Wilkinson at St. Louis. Enclosed with it was a letter from Mrs. Pike, the last word he

[6] It is probable that the Osage chief acquired the habit of using spoons from the Chouteaus, who for many years enjoyed exclusive trade with the Osage. In 1794, Pierre Chouteau and his brother Auguste erected a post in what is now Bates County, Missouri. A few years later they were given, by the Spanish government, the exclusive right to trade with these Indians for a period of six years. At the expiration of this time, Pierre Chouteau persuaded the Osage to move to the Arkansas River. For many years the Chouteaus were virtual "godfathers" to the Osage, teaching them many of the customs of civilized society.—*Dictionary of American History*, I, 370; Tixier, *op. cit.*, 126.

was to have from his family for another full year. No copy of Clara's letter has survived, but she evidently told her husband that she and the children had been ill.[7] A few days after his receipt of this letter, one of the Pike children died and was buried at Bellefontaine, but the Lieutenant was not to learn of this tragedy until his return the following year.

Wilkinson's letter contained some interesting remarks. "In regards to your approximation to the Spanish settlements, should your route lead you near them, or should you fall in with any of their parties, your conduct must be marked by such circumspection and direction as may prevent alarm or conflict, as you will be held responsible for consequences. On this subject I refer you to your orders."

The last statement has given the critics of Pike considerable ammunition, but whether Wilkinson referred to alleged secret orders, as suspected by Coues and others, must remain a mystery.

Further evidence of Wilkinson's duplicity is found elsewhere in the same letter. Pike was to be careful what he wrote to the Secretary of War, but "to me you may, and must write fully and freely, giving a minute detail of everything worthy of note. It is interesting to you to reach Nachitoches in season to be at the seat of government pending the session of Congress, yet you must not sacrifice any essential object of this point."

Does this mean that Wilkinson and Pike were "up to something"? To Pike's critics it suggests that his Arkansas expedition was part of the Wilkinson-Burr plot. But to his champions, the evidence appears so vague as to be neglible.

[7] Wilkinson's letter to Pike, August 6, 1806, concludes with the following remark: "Your children have been indisposed; but Mrs. Pike writes you. She appears well."

On August 21, Pike, at his camp near Grand Osage, held a council with the representatives from the Great and Little Osage tribes.[8] After making a speech explaining their new status within the United States, he distributed medals and gifts and then requested horses for his overland journey to the Pawnee and Kansas Indians.

At first the Osage were reluctant to supply the Americans, and their hesitancy forced Pike to make exhorbitant offers for the animals. Eventually fifteen horses were purchased or rented, and thirty warriors and chiefs were persuaded to accompany the party. Both the animals and the Indians soon proved a burden. Many of the horses, of poor quality, gave out along the trail, or else the owner insisted on turning back before the journey's end.

Unfortunately the elation and gratitude of the Osage at the return of their people was of short duration. Soon after Pike left, they were complaining to the Indian agent at St. Louis that their American father had forgotten them. According to White Hair, one of the Osage chiefs, Pike had promised him that his nation would be brought together, that a mill would be built in his village and regular trade established. None of these things had been done. Furthermore, White Hair maintained, Pike had purchased horses and supplies for which no one would pay, and the prisoners had not all been returned. Also, Lieutenant Wilkinson, one of Pike's party, had taken seven horses without paying for them.

The validity of these charges is hard to ascertain. William

---

[8] The Little Osage were subordinated to the Great Osage. Two years before Pike's visit, the explorers Lewis and Clark had found the Great Osage, numbering about five hundred warriors, in a village on the south bank of the Osage River. The Little Osage, numbering about half as many, lived in a village some six miles distant.—Frederick Webb Hodge, (ed.), *Handbook of American Indians*, Part 2, 158.

Clark, brigadier general and Indian agent at St. Louis, wrote the Secretary of War nearly a year after Pike had passed through the Osage country that "Traders in the neighborhood give very unpleasant news of Mr. Pike."[9] Apparently his dealing with the Osage did more harm than good.

On August 26, before Pike took leave of this nation, he sold one of his boats for one hundred dollars in merchandise and left the other in care of Chief Wind. The Americans now took to their horses, and the expedition became characteristically a Plains journey, the shallow river forcing them to stay on land. "Pike is now fairly enroute," according to Coues.[10]

Six days of riding brought them to the ridge in southeastern Kansas dividing the tributary waters of the Missouri from those of the Arkansas. Pike described the view from the divide as sublime. "The prairie rising and falling in regular swells, as far as the sight can extend, produces a very beautiful appearance." At the top of a gravel-covered knoll, he rested on his horse and with one full sweep surveyed the surrounding country, watching the shadows of the hills race across the intervening valleys. With a last look at the Osage River, he moved on to establish camp at the foot of the ridge. Just beyond were the burning wind-swept plains, the "Great American Desert."

Keeping together his Indian companions, "a faithless set of poltroons," was one of Pike's chief concerns as the party pushed across Kansas. The route now pursued lay in a northwesterly direction, and save for the ever present herds of buffalo and the growing dissatisfaction of the Osage, was not particular interesting. Game was so plentiful that one hunter

[9] William Clark to Henry Dearborn, May 18, 1807, John Sibley Papers (typed copy), Missouri Historical Society.
[10] Coues, *op. cit.*, II, 394.

could easily support two hundred men a day, and the soldiers had to be restrained from mere sportive shooting of the buffalo. Nor were buffalo the only game. "I stood on a hill," Pike observed, "and in one view below me saw buffalo, elk, deer, antelope, and panther."

As Pike led the first American expedition across the middle plains of the United States, he was moved to make a prophecy since frequently quoted. "This vast plains of the western hemisphere may become in time as celebrated as the sandy deserts of Africa; for I saw in my route, in various places, tracts of many leagues where the wind had thrown up the sand in all the fanciful form of the ocean's rolling wave, and on which not a speck of vegetable matter existed." It was this statement, and a similar one made by Major Stephen Long in 1820, that helped create the myth of a "Great American Desert."[11]

Explorers who had preceded Pike and Long had also described the region as a desert. In 1541, the credulous Spanish explorer, Coronado, had crossed this vast area in search of Quivira, the legendary city of gold, while another Spaniard, De Soto, was approaching its eastern edge. Practically all who crossed them, from Coronado to Horace Greeley, felt that they had to find an explanation for the Great Plains.

Lieutenant Pike later reported to General Wilkinson one national advantage that might arise from these immense prairies: they would be the means of restricting the population to some certain limits, thereby insuring the permanence of the Union. "Our citizens being so prone to rambling and extending themselves on the frontier, will, through necessity, be constrained to limit their extent on the west to the borders of the Missouri and Mississippi, while they leave the prairies, in-

[11] For many years maps of the United States labeled the Great Plains as "The Great American Desert."

capable of cultivation, to the wandering and uncivilized aborigines of the country."[12]

Indeed, who could have envisioned in 1806 those changes to be wrought here by the great cattle drives from Texas, railroads, barbed wire, windmills, dry farming, and modern hydroelectric projects?

On September 22, Pike first learned from a Pawnee hunter that a party of three hundred Spaniards had lately come as far as the Sabine River, but for what purpose he was unable to discover. The Pawnee also spoke of war between the Comanche, Pawnee, and Kansas—doubtless causing the Lieutenant's heart to beat faster at the thought of his troubles ahead. A few days later, just before entering the first Pawnee village, Pike and his party crossed the path of these Spanish dragoons.

Their presence was no surprise, and he should have had no doubt about their purposes. Indeed, General Wilkinson had warned him that agents at St. Louis might inform the Spaniards of his expedition. In fact, Spanish officials had learned of Pike's intention before he left the city and had vainly sought to intercept him.

On reaching the outskirts of the Pawnee village on September 25, Pike and his party were met by a reception committee and received a formal welcome after the Pawnee custom. Pike then accompanied Chief White Wolf to the center of the village, while his soldiers and Osage companions passed around the lodges and encamped on the Republican River a

[12] Professor Walter Prescott Webb, the Great Plains historian, comments that we are apt to smile at Pike's prophecy, but that in a sense it was fulfilled: "The American people were restricted, and their movement westward was temporarily arrested. It is entirely possible, if we also resort to speculation, that the Great Plains did after all preserve the Union by limiting the expansion of the cotton kingdom."—*The Great Plains*, 156.

short distance away. White Wolf proved a genial host and extremely vocal for an Indian. After a warm dinner he proceeded to give Pike all details of his recent visit with the Spaniards.

It would seem that when the Spanish governor of Chihuahua had learned of Pike's contemplated expedition, he had sent a Lieutenant Malgares[13] with six hundred mounted troops from Santa Fé to find and arrest him. The Spanish force consisted of one hundred regular troops and five hundred New Mexico militia, all mounted on white horses, except Malgares and two principal officers, who were on jet-black ones. Malgares' mission into the Louisiana region, in addition to intercepting Pike, was to drive out the unauthorized traders and settlers, either forcing them to retire to the United States or taking them to Santa Fé as prisoners. Also, the Spanish expedition was to explore the region between Santa Fé and the acknowledged western boundaries of the United States, to visit with various western tribes and "renew the chains of ancient amity" which had previously existed between the Plains Indians and the Spaniards.

About the middle of June, 1806, Malgares and his dragoons set out from Santa Fé. His mounted force and extra horses and mules must have formed an imposing cavalcade for the time and place.[14] The course pursued at first, according to Pike's published journal, was the Red River from its source toward its mouth.[15] Several meetings were held en route with

[13] Lieutenant Don Facundo Malgares, who had already distinguished himself in several expeditions against the Apache and other tribes of the Southwest, later became a close friend to Pike. The American officer was to record in his journal that Malgares was one of the few Spanish officers whom he encountered who was still loyal to the Spanish king in 1807. Malgares is remembered in the history of New Mexico as its *ad interim* governor from 1819 to 1820.

[14] The Spaniards carried provisions for six months; their livestock and horses totaled approximately two thousand animals.

[15] If Malgares actually came down the Red River, as Pike's maps and

important bands of Comanche, and a profound impression was made by the colorful Spaniards.

After descending the river for a distance of 233 leagues, Malgares turned north and struck across the plains to the Arkansas. Misfortune dogged his progress: mutiny broke out among the New Mexican militia, but was successfully repressed; a wandering band of Pawnee stole part of the livestock; and many of the horses became lame. Approximately half of the men and animals were eventually left behind, and with the remainder the Spanish commander pressed on to the country of the Pawnee, arriving there about one month ahead of Pike.

"There is profound significance," writes H. M. Chittenden, "in the almost simultaneous presence of these two expeditions upon the boundless prairies that separated the frontier settlements of their respective countries. One was looking into the future and paving a way for the irresistible expansion of his people. The other was clinging to the past and watching the wild inhabitants of the plains and seeking with presents and speeches and grandiloquent pictures of the greatness of their respective nations, to secure their attachment. In this preliminary skirmish between two powers, which were even then, did they but know it, preparing the way for inevitable conflict, the advantage was on the side of the Spaniards. Between the powerful and well-appointed expedition of Malarges and the

journals clearly show, then it becomes evident (or reasonably so) that the Spaniards knew of the headwaters of the Red long before Pike's expedition of 1806, and much longer before the exploratory work of Marcy in 1852. This is deduced from the fact that Malgares followed a well-beaten wagon road across a plain and down the Red to a point opposite the great bend of the Arkansas before turning northward. However, most recent historians who have investigated this field maintain that Malgares really descended the present Canadian River and that the true sources of the Red were never explored until 1852. This latter assertion may be true, but the proof is circumstantial.

small and poorly equipped handful of men with Pike the contrast was great, and to the untutored mind of the prairie inhabitant, there could be no doubt of the outcome of a trial of strength between their governments. He could not see the forces behind those outward manifestations—the expanding vigor of a young nation and the decadent energies of the old; but in due time he came to know."[16]

Malgares remained at the Pawnee settlements for several days. While there, he held a council with the Pawnee chiefs of northern Kansas and southern Nebraska, distributing medals and flags, and making a lasting impression on the Indians. After taking into custody several American traders found in the region, the Spanish commander retraced his route to Santa Fé, which he reached early in October. There he remained until Lieutenant Pike was eventually captured by Spanish forces and ordered to Mexico—Malgares acting as his escort through the Spanish provinces.

During his two weeks at the Pawnee villages, Pike tried to effect peace settlements with the tribes of the region; and although he had some success with the Osage and the Kansas, the Pawnee proved exceedingly difficult. They were reluctant to surrender their Spanish flags and medals, and only agreed in the end to an exchange of the Spanish flags for ours. Pike then returned them the Spanish flag, for, as he said, "I did not wish to embarrass them with the Spaniards whom I feared might return there in force." This act of diplomacy was greeted with "general shouts of applause."

In 1806, at the time of Pike's visit to the Pawnee, as many as thirty separate tribes dwelt on the Great Plains. The Pawnee belonged to the great Caddoan family and originally were

[16] *History of the American Fur Trade,* 495–96.

sedentary. According to legend, they once lived "upon the Red River, below the mouth of the Washita," in eastern Oklahoma or Arkansas, whence they migrated northward. In time they split into several bands, some proceeded northward and settled on the Platte, while others moved westward and established themselves on the Republican River.[17] It was this band that Pike visited on his western journey.[18]

Pike reported that the Pawnee, like the Osage and the Kansas, were raising corn (maize), watermelon, beans, and pumpkins—at least enough corn and pumpkins each year to thicken their soup. However, the buffalo continued to furnish them most of the necessities of life. They gathered their corn each summer and dried it in the sun. Their pumpkins, cut into very small slices, were preserved in much the same manner. Part of the food was then buried, and a fire was built over the spot to conceal the fresh dirt and so prevent theft. It will be remembered that Pike had hidden part of his supplies in just this way on his Mississippi expedition.

During the winter months the Pawnee, like the Osage and other Plains Indians, moved from their dirt houses into tepees. The latter, surprisingly enough, were much warmer when properly constructed with an inner wall. This additional wall left an air space that served as insulation, so that a small fire was all that was necessary to keep the interior warm in cold weather.

Pike describes the construction of the Pawnee houses very

---

[17] Waldo Rudolph Wedel, *An Introduction to Pawnee Archeology*, 7.

[18] The exact location of the Pawnee village where Pike camped has never been determined. That there were several Pawnee villages in this region and that the Republican River crosses the present Kansas-Nebraska line in practically an east-west direction, has added to the uncertainty. Coues expresses the opinion that Pike's camp on the Republican River was in present Nebraska and not in Kansas, as is generally believed.

clearly. First, a circular hole was dug, approximately sixty feet in diameter and four feet deep. Around the edge was set a row of posts extending about five feet above the ground, forming a solid wall when smaller limbs were interlaced. An inner circle of poles, ten or twelve feet in height, formed a central ring of about ten feet in diameter. Long poles were then laid on, slanting upward from the lower to the higher row of uprights, leaving a small opening at the top to let out smoke.

The roof would then be thatched with grass or small limbs and covered with about two feet of dirt. Dirt, too, was piled against the outside wall until it reached the eaves, giving the whole structure the appearance of a little cone-shaped hill. Last of all was built the entrance, consisting of two walls of upright poles and a flat roof covered with grass and dirt. Usually about six feet long and three feet wide, it made a hall-like entryway.

These buildings, Pike observed, were fairly comfortable, and the partitions inside allowed some degree of privacy. Like the Osage, the Pawnee arranged their lodges in a great circle, forming a stockade for their horses.

Although the Comanche and Apache perhaps are better-known Plains Indians, the Pawnee have received unusual attention.[19] It helped that their name was easily pronounced and remembered. Also, since they lived near what later became the Santa Fé Trail, they came into frequent contact with wagon trains, and were often blamed for raids actually committed by other tribes.[20] Pike said that they were the only natives of the plains who went into battle on foot instead of mounted, a cir-

---

[19] We find the earliest historic reference to the Pawnee in the journals of Coronado's expedition to the Great Plains in 1541.

[20] The Sioux were to suffer the same reputation in connection with the wagon trains that later went to Oregon and California.

117

cumstance which also drew attention to them. That the Pawnee were the first Plains Indians to use firearms gave them an early advantage over their tribal enemies.[21]

However, one of their ceremonies included a human sacrifice. The victim was usually a girl, young, healthy, and a virgin. Captured from a rival tribe, she would be kept by herself, fattened on the best food, and treated with great kindness, never informed that she was soon to die. After several weeks, the final ceremony of fasting and dancing would begin. Then, on the fourth day, the maiden was painted all over, half red and half white. Four warriors escorted her to the end of the village, where a scaffold had been set up. All of the men, women, and children would gather around the victim while she was tied, spread-eagle, on the scaffold. A huge fire was built underneath, but before the flames could reach the maiden, a warrior would shoot her through the heart with an arrow. Everyone then passed their hands through the flames and smoke and rubbed their bodies, while praying for good crops and good health.[22]

It soon became apparent to Lieutenant Pike that he and his men were no longer wanted at the Pawnee settlement, despite the warmth of their first reception. In fact, Spanish flattery and show had so impressed the Indians that they scoffed at Pike and his wretched soldiers as but sorry representatives of a major power. When the Americans prepared to leave, the

[21] "Through all of the vicissitudes of the 19th century the Pawnee never made war against the U. S. On the contrary they gave many evidences of forbearance under severe provocation by waiting, under their treaty agreement, for the Government to right their wrongs, while Pawnee scouts faithfully and courageously served in the U. S. army during Indian hostilities."—Hodge, *op. cit.*, 214.

[22] Pike does not mention witnessing such a ceremony, but it was known to exist among the Pawnee as late as 1838.

chief of the Pawnee informed Pike that he had promised to halt any American party planning to cross the plains, and that if they insisted on continuing, he and his braves would have to stop them.

Pike replied that the warriors of the Great Father were not women to be turned back with words, that they had been sent out to explore the western country and make peace with the Indians. He then left the village and returned to camp, "considerably perturbed."

A week later the Americans were ready to push on, having obtained more horses in the meantime, although at an exhorbitant price. It was in this interval that Pike learned from a French trader that Lewis and Clark had lately returned to St. Louis from the mouth of the Columbia. The trader had met their expedition on the Missouri a few weeks earlier, and had informed them in turn of Pike's expedition on its way across the middle plains.

As Pike and his company departed for the Arkansas, they took a circular route around the village to avoid attack by the Pawnee. "We made every arrangement to make them pay as dearly for the attempt as possible," the Lieutenant wrote, but the men were ordered to hold their fire until the enemy were within five or six paces.

"I believe it would cost them at least 100 men to have exterminated us, which would have been necessary," commented Pike. However, the Pawnee, seeing that the whites were ready for them, made no serious effort to stop them, and the expedition continued unmolested.

The course which Pike and his crew now took followed what later became the famous Santa Fé Trail. Day by day they pushed on, most of their Osage companions having already turned back. Three warriors and an Indian woman were

119

all that remained of the party of thirty Indians which had accompanied the expedition from Grand Osage.

Their march across the plains of Kansas, almost due south, was without incident except for the sighting of some sixty Pawnee on a hunting expedition. On discovering them, Pike expected trouble, but he soon perceived they were merely chasing a herd of elk. With astonishing skill the Pawnee rode among the fleeing animals and "buried their arrows up to the plume," killing them almost instantly.

A few days more brought them to the Arkansas River. This stream was monotonously uniform, its sandy banks low and steep, its bed, quicksand. Here Pike and his party halted and built an encampment near present-day Larned, Kansas. This was the designated spot at which the party must divide, Lieutenant Wilkinson with his group to descend the Arkansas to Fort Adams, while Pike led the remainder to the source of the same stream. Accordingly Pike ordered the necessary preparations.

10

"Three Cheers to the Mexican Mountains"

THE explorers remained encamped on the Arkansas for several days while canoes were constructed for Lieutenant Wilkinson and his small group, who were to descend the stream. Meanwhile, Pike and three or four companions explored the surrounding country and hunted buffalo and deer. They were eager to pick up the trail of the Spaniards who had passed along the same route a few weeks earlier, for this trail would lead to Santa Fé.

The Lieutenant made a careful observation of the prairie-dog towns scattered widely on the plains, particularly along the Arkansas. These small rodents were called "wistonwash" by the Indians, but Pike preferred the name "prairie squirrel," for they looked more like squirrels than anything else he had seen.[1]

---

[1] The contrast between a squirrel that climbed trees in the East and one that burrowed in the ground in the West was too much for most travelers who crossed the plains after Pike. Consequently, the prairie squirrel was made a dog! "If them things was called by their right name," an old stage driver once remarked, "there would not be one left in the country."

It should be pointed out, too, that the French called these creatures *chiens* (dogs) long before the Americans reached the plains.

Their villages were generally on an elevated spot, close to water, and might extend over as much as two square miles, with burrows every ten or twelve steps. Pike maintained that these burrows were dug in a spiral form with two or three animals dwelling in each—often in company with rattlesnakes, horned toads, and tortoises. There would be no vegetation in such a town, the ground being smooth and bare save for the mounds of dirt thrown up around the entrances. After pouring 140 kettles of water into one of these holes, the Americans were still unable to drive out any of its inhabitants. Thereupon Pike concluded that the various burrows were connecting, and gave up trying to capture any of the live animals.

However, several prairie dogs were killed, and it was discovered that the meat, when exposed to frost for a night or two, had an excellent flavor. Shooting these animals was almost as difficult as taking them alive: "As you approach their town, you are saluted on all sides with the cry 'wishtonwash' from which they derive their name with the Indians, uttered in a shrill and piercing manner. You then observe them all retreating to the entrance of their burrows, where they post themselves, and regard every movement you make. It requires a nice shot with a rifle to kill them, as they must be killed dead, for as long as life exists they continued to work into their cells."

At ten o'clock on October 28, 1806, Lieutenant Wilkinson, four privates, and the sole remaining Osage departed in two canoes, newly constructed of buffalo skins and green cottonwood. Carrying twenty-one days' provisions with them, they expected to reach the Mississippi within two or three weeks, but it was not until seventy-three days later that Wilkinson finally achieved his destination. His journey down the Arkansas was the first American expedition through what is now Oklahoma.

On the same date Pike and his remaining companions again took up the trail of western exploration, their immediate objective the source of this same stream, the Arkansas.

Day by day Pike ascended the winding river, pushing farther and farther into the sea of plains, a region previously unexplored by Americans. Near what is now Fort Dodge the party sighted a herd of wild horses. From this point on, Pike was to observe many such herds, sometimes containing several thousand animals in a single group.

In an effort to capture some of the horses, Pike and his men first tried the common method of creasing, a feat that required an expert marksman, able to hit the animal along the nape of the neck, close to his vertebra. If the shot were properly placed, the horse would be temporarily stunned, thus giving his pursuers an opportunity to seize and hold him. When this method yielded no success, they tried to rope some of the animals, but the mustangs proved too swift, and in flight left the men far behind.[2]

Farther on, the explorers discovered great herds of buffalo, deer, and elk moving toward the mountains in the wake of the onrushing winter. One herd of buffalo covered the entire prairie as far as the eye could see. "I believe that there are buffalo, elk, and deer sufficient on the banks of the Arkansas alone, if used without waste," Pike observed, "to feed all the savages in the United States territory one century."

By mid-November the cold north winds were "hedge-hopping" across the rolling plains with increasing severity. The grass grew thinner as the men proceeded westward, and when snow began to fall, there was nothing for the horses to

---

[2] It is generally assumed that the mustang descended from horses brought to America by the Spaniards in the sixteenth century.

eat but the bark and leaves of small cottonwood trees, which the men cut each night.

For several weeks now, their horses half-starved, Pike and his small band of soldiers had ridden deeper into the vast, unknown region. Each day had been like the one before, but on November 15, 1806, Pike sighted on the far western horizon that "small blue cloud" that was to give him immortality and make his name known to every schoolboy in subsequent generations. Rising out of the plains to the northwest towered a tremendous mountain, above a chain of lesser, though mighty, peaks. With one accord the party gave "three cheers to the Mexican Mountains," for Pike thought these mountains presented a natural boundary between the provinces of Louisiana and New Mexico. And, although he fancied himself nearer, he was still more than 150 miles from the range.

For the next several days the American followed the course of the Arkansas toward the northwest. Each day brought renewed hardships; and the mountains that had once appeared so near would now often seem farther off than when first sighted. One by one the horses fell, exhausted, and had to be abandoned. Soon less than half of the animals were fit for use. Every night was colder than the one before. Finally, Pike decided to halt and lay in a supply of meat before proceeding farther.

After several buffalo had been killed and the meat dried, the party pushed on again. A day or two later they experienced perhaps the most anxious moments of the journey. Before realizing what had happened, they found themselves surrounded by an army of Pawnee. However, as the Indians approached, Pike observed that part of them were unarmed and concluded that an immediate attack was not intended.

He was just dismounting, thinking the Pawnee wished to

smoke a peace pipe, when one of the red men dashed forward, seized Pike's horse, mounted it, and rode away at full speed. Then the other Indians, rushed up, surrounded the Americans, and insisted on embracing them most affectionately. Never before had Pike or his men witnessed such behavior on the part of Indians.

After a short while the confusion subsided, the Lieutenant's horse was returned to him, and the Indians made signs for a parley. A large circle was formed—Indians and Americans sitting side by side. Pike distributed gifts to the chief and several of his warriors, which they readily accepted. Indeed, they demanded more, and when further presents were not forthcoming, their temper changed at once. Some threw away their gifts in anger.

Pike then ordered his men to load and make ready to depart, but once again the Pawnee surrounded the soldiers, this time, instead of embracing them, brazenly stealing every article in sight. Pike's pistols were of special interest to several of the braves, who boldly tried to lay hold of them. At first, the Lieutenant patiently resisted their advances; then, as his efforts failed, he vainly appealed to the chief to order his men to behave. After that, believing his situation greatly endangered, Pike ordered his men to withdraw from the Indians.

He then addressed the warriors in a manner that left no doubt of his intentions—he promised to kill the next man who touched an article belonging to the whites. This stern warning had its proper effect. Both parties went at once on their separate ways, in opposite directions and without further conversation.[3] As for the Americans, they considered themselves extremely fortunate in escaping without serious mishap.

[3] The site of Pike's encounter with the Pawnee is near the spot where the Santa Fe Railroad crosses the Arkansas River.

One day's march farther brought them to the site of Pueblo, Colorado, where Pike determined to establish a fortified camp, from which he could make an expedition into the "blue mountains." These, he thought, could be reached in a day, and from the pinnacle he might map the country.

The next day they started building the log stockade, five feet high. Its exact location has not been fixed exactly, and even in 1820, when Major Stephen H. Long visited the region, he was unable to find any trace of it. Very probably it was washed away soon after it was abandoned, since the Arkansas here is subject to frequent floods.

After the structure was completed, Pike, Dr. Robinson, and two privates left camp, intending to reach the foot of the great mountain, apparently a short distance to the north, before the end of that day. The towering peak loomed straight ahead, but before the travelers could approach it, they had to cross a range extending parallel to its base, now called the Cheyenne Mountains. Not, indeed, until the third day did they reach Cheyenne Mountain, immediately south of the peak.

Abandoning their baggage and provisions, the four men began to climb, only to find their task increasingly difficult. When darkness approached, they were still some distance from the summit and took refuge in a cave, without food, blankets, or water. The temperature fell below zero, and before morning the surrounding country lay deep in new snow.

Although the night had been a sleepless one, the sore and hungry Americans renewed their climb at the first glimmer of dawn. This day was November 27, 1806—Thanksgiving Day, Pike recalled—and the breath-taking spectacle spread out below as he looked back made him feel for the first time some compensation for the ordeal of the past few days and nights.[4]

From the top of Cheyenne Mountain they had now an
unobstructed view of the peak beyond in all its majestic gran-
deur. But its towering summit was still some twelve miles
away (as the crow flies), bare of timber and covered with ice
and snow, with a valley between it and them. "It was as high
again as what we had ascended, and it would have taken a
whole day's march to arrive at its base, when I believe no
human being could have ascended to its pinical," said Pike.

As Pike stood up to his waist in snow, the temperature
four degrees below zero, without proper clothing, it doubtless
did not occur to him that all his life he had been slowly but
surely approaching this spot. As has been said before, this
moment was, literally, the peak of his career. Tremendously
impressed and excited by the "Grand Peak," Pike nevertheless realized the foolhardiness of trying to go farther. The
men had had no food for two days. Their cotton clothing was
more than inadequate, and their strength was almost gone.
To proceed further would be suicide. Slowly, Pike turned back.

It is generally but erroneously believed today that Lieutenant Pike was the first American to scale the great peak in
Colorado which is an enduring monument to his memory. Such
a feat would have been practically impossible under the conditions he encountered in midwinter, 1806. Nevertheless, his
prophecy that the mountain could never be climbed was re-
futed before many years had passed. In 1820, Dr. Edwin
James and three other members of Major Long's Rocky
Mountain expedition did reach the summit. Conditions were
then very different, however, for James, properly equipped,
accomplished the feat in midsummer.

Long recorded in his notes for July 15, 1820, the following comment on the peak: "From information derived from

[4] Probably Pike was now gazing upon present Colorado Springs.

the Indians and hunters who have frequently visited this part of the country, and also from the account given by Pike, relative to the peak, it appears that no person, either civilized or savage, had ever ascended to its summit, and that the ascent was deemed utterly impracticable. Dr. James having accomplished this difficult and laborious task, I have thought proper to call the peak after his name, as a compliment to which his zeal and perseverance, together with the skillful attention with which he has examined its characters and productions, gives him the fairest claim. Pike has indeed given us notice that there is such a peak, but he only saw it at a distance; the unfavorable circumstances under which he came into its neighborhood preventing his arrival even at its base. He attempted to ascertain its altitude,[5] but it is believed his estimate is very erroneous."[6]

In referring to the famous peak in his journal and on his maps, Pike called it "Grand Peak." He did not name it in honor of himself, as is commonly believed, and for several decades it was called "Pike's Peak" by some, "James' Peak" by others.

When John C. Frémont explored the Rockies in 1843 and 1844, he labeled the famous mountain "Pike's Peak" on his maps and consistently referred to it by that name in his reports. On July 12, 1894, Governor Alva Adams of Colorado, in an address to the students and faculty of Colorado College, at Colorado Springs, gave the following account of the naming of the peak: "The name of Pike's Peak begins to appear in the literature of the prairies and mountains about the middle of the century, but it was not irrevocably christened until the

[5] Long estimated the altitude of the peak at 11,507½ feet; Pike's estimate was 18,561. The accepted height today is 14,110 feet above sea level.
[6] Edwin James, *Account of an Expedition From Pittsburgh to the Rocky Mountains*, in Thwaites, *Early Western Travels*, XVI, 36.

Pike's Peak gold excitement [1859], when the name was fixed to remain as long as men love to listen to stories of valor."

No one can deny Pike his honor as the first Anglo-American to gaze upon Pike's Peak, but the Spaniards knew of it long before him, and Pike himself records that it served them as a boundary for their northwestern travel out of Santa Fé. He found, too, that the Indian nations, for hundreds of miles around, spoke of it with admiration.

On a clear day Pike's Peak is sometimes visible for 150 miles or more. It is often referred to as the most famous mountain in the world, although there are twenty-seven higher peaks in Colorado alone. Pike's Peak, however, rises boldly from the plains where all may see it. "In our wanderings in the mountains," Pike wrote in 1807, "it was never out of sight except when in a valley."

When Pike and his three companions got back to their stockade on November 29, faint with hunger and fatigue, distressing circumstances awaited them. For several days a snow storm had been raging, so that the supply of meat was now practically exhausted, and the horses, unable to obtain grass, were near starvation.

Pike decided to push on into the mountains as soon as the storm subsided, which was three days later. He now contemplated three immediate objectives: to pick up the lost Spanish trail, to determine the source of the Arkansas, and to find the Red River. Three days of difficult travel brought the party to the mouth of the now famous Royal Gorge in Colorado. Pitching camp nearby at the site of Cañon City,[7] Pike sent out several scouting parties to search for the trail of the Spanish dragoons, believed to have passed through a few weeks earlier.

[7] Cañon City is the home of the Colorado State Penitentiary today.

When all had failed, he decided to leave the Arkansas and continue to the northwest, deeper into the mountains. Some days later, on December 13, he reached a stream which he supposed to be the South Platte, a correct assumption, as he later discovered.

Five days hence and after traveling southward, another stream was encountered, which Pike believed to be the Red River and determined to explore to its source. With two of his men he now took leave of the party, ordering them to descend the newly discovered stream. He meanwhile ascended the river for several days toward the northwest, a difficult journey as it proved, for the stream often twisted through narrow canyons, and its banks were thick with yellow pine and cedar.

Eventually, on reaching a high point near the river, Pike obtained a view of the surrounding country. Following the stream with his eye for a distance of thirty miles, he now realized that its source could be attained only with much time and difficulty. Reluctantly, he concluded that there was nothing to be gained by proceeding farther and turned back to overtake the main party, slowly retreating out of the mountains toward the southeast.

On December 24, they rejoined the expedition, only to learn that its members had suffered many hardships. Not one of the sixteen was properly clothed for the sub-zero weather, and food supplies were now very low. At night the weary travelers had to sleep on the wet ground, without blankets, for most of the bedding had long since gone into socks. Their only defense against the freezing night air was to build huge fires and lie as close to them as possible. Here "one side burned while the other was pierced by cold winds."

Christmas Day was observed in an atmosphere of depression, while Pike decided to abondon his search for the Spanish trail and to return to the plains via the stream on which he was encamped. His horses now either dead or useless, he ordered construction of sleds for the transport of supplies. A few days downstream, on January 5, 1807, Pike, from the summit of a hill, discovered to his surprise that the river he had been following broke out of the mountains at the same pass he had first seen a month earlier. This was in fact the outlet of the Arkansas —the river Pike had supposed to be the Red.

Save for the comforting knowledge that he had seen the source of the Arkansas, one objective of his expedition, Pike was much disconcerted at this discovery. He remembered, meanwhile, that it was his twenty-eighth birthday and he hoped never to spend another under such trying circumstances.

Pike's men received the news of their present position in disappointed silence. With heavy heart they continued downstream to their previous camp site of December 10 (Cañon City). Here, it was decided, after a brief consultation, to build another stockade, to lay in a supply of meat for those unable to travel because of frozen feet, and then to march toward the south. Accordingly a stockade was erected, and on January 14, Pike and the thirteen men still fit for travel, each carrying a load of seventy pounds, took leave of their two disabled comrades. They now proposed to cross the range of mountains to the south (Sangre de Cristo) and on the other side select a camp site where the weather would be warmer and the game more plentiful.

Coues, who finds in Pike's every move evidence of secret orders from Wilkinson, notes that the Lieutenant was here "brave to excess." Otherwise he would never have tried to penetrate these mountains under such trying conditions. "If he had to hunt for the unknown source of a river which came eastward from there, he would have backed out of the mountains, gone down the Arkansas a piece, struck south at his convenience till he found that river, and then considered the chances of being able to follow it up to its source. That Red River of which Pike is supposed to have gone in search was never found, for the simple reason that there is no such river in that part of the world—as Pike himself knew."[8]

This argument, though logical, is not conclusive. Actually Pike had no way of knowing where the source of the Red River was, and, in the light of our present knowledge, his real objective at this time remains a mystery.

If they had known hardships before, those discomforts were as nothing to the ones to come. Nine of Pike's men soon got their feet so badly frozen that they could not walk. Worse yet, the supply of meat was again exhausted, and buffalo and deer were not to be seen. On January 18, in a temperature eighteen degree below zero, the Lieutenant, with Dr. Robinson and two soldiers, left their comrades to go in search of game.

Although they sighted a herd of buffalo, not one of the hunters could kill one. Unable to sleep for cold at night, his thin body almost exhausted, Pike nearly resolved to die in solitude rather than return to camp and witness the sufferings of his men. Yet he and Dr. Robinson doggedly went on with the hunt.

Suddenly a lone buffalo crossed their path. "By the greatest of luck, the first shot stopped him." The animal was speedily butchered, and Pike and Robinson, for their two companions by now had returned to camp, loaded as much as they could on their backs and rejoined their party. "When I threw my

[8] Coues, *op. cit.*, II, 481, n. 28.

load down," Pike remarked in his journal, "I was attacked with a giddiness of the head, which lasted for some minutes." However, a sumptuous feast soon followed, and high spirits prevailed among the men.

When it was decided to continue the march, two more of the party proved not sufficiently recovered from frost-bite to travel. Reluctantly the others pushed forward through three feet of snow, leaving their entire supply of buffalo meat for their sick comrades. Soon their plight was as bad as before. A raging snow storm spoiled the hunting, but the Lieutenant pushed grimly on, and his men began to complain.

One of the soldiers averred it was "more than human nature could bear, to march three days without sustenance through snow three feet deep, to carry burdens only fit for horses." When a short time later a buffalo was killed and butchered and its meat had restored the morale of his men, Pike felt it time to rebuke the soldier for his words. The offender was called up and in the presence of the others severely reproved. Furthermore, Pike warned him, if he uttered another such seditious statement, the punishment would be death by a firing squad. If this action appears unduly harsh, allowance must be made for the desperate circumstances and the need of discipline.

No man of the party had been less selfish or more self-sacrificing than Pike himself. Yet some of his critics have marveled that his men did not complain more than they did. They contend that the party's predicament and the great hardships they were called upon to bear were due solely to Pike's rash choosing of a winter journey through this mountain wilderness.

Apparently his late experiences had had a sobering effect upon the young commander, for he resolved never to march again with so few provisions. Happily he succeeded in a short time in killing three more buffalo, whose meat was dried on scaffolds and made ready for transport. Meanwhile, still another man of the party became so crippled with frozen feet that they had to leave him. Only ten of the party could still walk, but Pike was determined to cross the Sangre de Cristo Mountains before sending back for the five left behind.

On January 27 the weary travelers came to a small stream (Sand Creek) which they fervently hailed as the waters of the Red River. Following the ravine for several miles, they emerged from the mountains through a pass (Sand Hill) and entered what is now the San Luis Valley, in the basin of the Río Grande. From there they went southward, through the valley and along the stream. On both sides were mountain ranges, running north and south, while the valley itself was but a winding, narrow desert of rolling sand dunes.

From one of the larger dunes Pike, through his telescope, observed to his delight a large river in the west. The stream flowed south and appeared to be some fifteen miles distant. According to Pike's own account, which he consistently repeated, he believed that he had at last reached the elusive Red River. Whether he was then actually aware that he was gazing on the Río Grande instead may never be known.

In any case he proceeded southwest and reached the bank of the river on January 30. "As there was no timber here we determined on descending until we found timber, in order to make transports to descend the river with, where we might establish a position that four or five might defend against the insolence, cupidity, and barbarity of the savages, while the others returned to assist the poor fellows who had been left behind at different points."

Thirteen miles farther on, they reached the mouth of another stream flowing from the west.[9] Ascending this for about five miles, they stopped at a wooded area, and there built a stockade.

Pike's proponents maintain that he thought he was now encamped a few miles west of the Red River. A glance at a map will show that the source of the Red is in the Texas Panhandle, far south of the Lieutenant's actual position; but since this stream had not yet been explored by any Anglo-American, Pike may be forgiven his vagueness as to its whereabouts.[10]

Still he must have known that when he crossed over to the west bank of what he professed to believe was the Red River, he was violating Spanish territory. Hart and Hulbert championed the Lieutenant's cause on this point, arguing that he marked the Río Grande on his maps as "Red River," and had no opportunity to correct this error before the maps were taken from him by his Spanish captors.[11]

Several days of arduous labor were required for Pike and his men to complete the stockade west of the Río Grande. Heavy cottonwood logs two feet in diameter were first cut and laid on top of each other to form a rectangle about thirty-six feet square and six feet high. Smaller logs were then added to bring the works to a height of twelve feet.

A ditch was dug around the inside walls of the stockade, and long sharp stakes were set up, slanting from the ditch and

[9] The Río Conejos.

[10] Humboldt's map of New Spain, compiled from data in the city of Mexico in 1804, indicated that the Spaniards labored under the same error as Pike. They thought the sources of the Red to be some two or three hundred miles northwest of their true positions. Humboldt's map shows that the main Red was well known, yet the headwaters of the Canadian River (which flows into the Arkansas near Fort Smith) were believed to be, and were charted as, the northwest extension of the Red to within fifty miles of Pike's stockade on the Río Conejos.

[11] Stephen H. Hart and Archer Butler Hulbert (eds.), *Zebulon Pike's Arkansas Journal*, xcii.

extending two feet over the top of the walls, making the place harder for an enemy to storm. Further protection was afforded by a second ditch, four feet deep, extending along the outer sides. This ditch was filled with water by a connecting channel from the near-by river.

Pike's stockade had no roof over any part and no regular entrance gate. To get inside, one crawled over a board across the outer ditch and through a small tunnel under the wall nearest the river's edge. Portholes were cut in the logs about eight feet above the ground and a platform was put up for the men to stand on while firing or acting as sentinels. Here, the Lieutenant remarked, he would not have had the least fear in resisting an enemy force of a hundred, before attempting an escape under cover of darkness.

As soon as leisure permitted, Pike and Dr. Robinson went out to hunt buffalo and deer and incidentally to explore the surrounding region. The Lieutenant was so inspired by the beauty of the land that he was moved to an eloquence uncommon in his journal. From a near-by hill, he thought the distant mountains the sublimest sight ever offered to the eyes of man: "The great and lofty mountains, covered with eternal snows, seemed to surround the luxuriant vale, crowned with perennial flowers, like a terrestial paradise shut out from the view of man."

Not until February 7 did Pike decide to send back for the men still in the mountains, a task for which five soldiers volunteered. On that same day, Dr. Robinson departed for Santa Fé, which he and Pike believed was not far off. Now only five men, including Pike, remained at the stockade, and the Lieutenant took advantage of the quiet to rest and work over his maps, journal, and official reports and observations.

The role of Dr. Robinson and the reason for his presence

with the Pike party has remained a mystery. Robinson was a civilian doctor whom Wilkinson had allowed to accompany Pike when he departed from St. Louis in 1806.[12] Doubtless there was need of medical service on so hazardous a journey, but there were many physicians available in the regular army, and it is strange that none was appointed.

Regardless of Wilkinson's motive in sending the young physician, he proved a valuable addition to the party. Not only did he give medical aid to the men, but he was a resourceful and agreeable comrade, whose services would have been sorely missed. "As a gentleman and companion in danger, difficulties, and hardships, I in particular, and the expedition in generally, owe much to his exertions," Pike remarked.

There is less doubt about the cause of Robinson's leaving the expedition in February, 1807. He left the stockade intending to find the Spaniards, and his efforts were not in vain.

In regard to Robinson's departure, the purposes of Pike's western journey should be recalled. Obviously, Pike was disappointed in failing to overtake the Spanish dragoons in Louisiana territory; and his wanderings in the mountains of Colorado are proof to his critics that he was not as interested in exploring the Red River as in finding the Spaniards. Pike knew that if he ran across a party of them, he would probably be taken to Santa Fé for questioning. While there he could obtain information which General Wilkinson greatly desired.

But his failure to intercept, or to be intercepted by, Spanish troops now caused the Lieutenant to resort to other means of attracting attention to his whereabouts. Before leaving St.

[12] Dr. John Hamilton Robinson had moved to St. Louis from Virginia in 1804 as a young man of twenty-two. Although his career, other than his relations to the Pike expedition, is not important here, it should be noted that throughout his adult life he was a man about whom mystery and suspicion seemed to gather.

137

Louis, he had been entrusted with a claim from one William Morrison against a Creole trader, Baptiste La Lande, now living at Santa Fé. Morrison was a prosperous merchant who had lived in Pike's home county (Bucks) in Pennsylvania and had later moved to Kaskaskia, Illinois. During Pike's stay at Kaskaskia in 1804–1805, he had become acquainted with Morrison, who was also a close friend of Wilkinson's.

In 1804, Morrison had supplied La Lande with trade goods to take to Santa Fé, expecting to realize a handsome profit from the venture. La Lande, however, did not return, and Pike, so he claimed, had meanwhile promised Morrison to collect the money due him: "When on the frontier the idea suggested itself to us to make this claim a pretext for Robinson to visit Santa Fe. We therefore gave it the proper appearance, and he marched for that place. Our views were to gain a knowledge of the country, the prospect of trade, force, etc.; while, at the same time, our treaties with Spain guaranteed to him, as a citizen of the United States, the right of seeking the recovery of all just debts or demands before the legal and authorized tribunals of the country."

Realizing that the claims in Robinson's hands "were is some degree spurious," the Lieutenant had no doubt that the Spaniards would pay him a call soon after Robinson's appearance at Santa Fé. He and his four companions now waited patiently at the stockade for these developments. They did not have to wait long before the expected visitors arrived.

11

"Is This Not the Red River?"

FEBRUARY 16, nine days after Robinson's departure, found Pike and one companion out hunting. About six miles from the stockade they sighted a deer and opened fire. The sound brought two horsemen from beyond the summit of a distant hill. Pike and the soldier now hurriedly reloaded, but the horsemen continued toward them, coursing at full speed across the intervening flat.

According to Pike's account, he and the soldier first made for a near-by woods hoping to evade their pursuers, but finding escape impossible, they stopped and prepared to make a stand; the horsemen halted about a hundred yards away. When Pike advanced toward them, they retired beyond gun range, but when he made for a ravine, the horsemen followed as fast as their horses could go.

"We suffered them to get within 40 yards where we had allured them; but they were about running off again, when I ordered the soldier to lay down his arms and walk toward them, at the same time standing ready with my rifle to kill either who would lift an arm in a hostile manner." Pike then called to the strangers that he and his companion were "Americans" and "friends."

It was with fear and trembling that the two horsemen now approached. They proved to be a Spanish dragoon and a civil-

139

ized Indian from Santa Fé. A short parley followed, during which Pike learned that Dr. Robinson had arrived at the city four days earlier. "As I knew them to be spies, I thought proper to inform them merely that I was about to descend the river to Nachitoches." The visitors, however, were not content with the Lieutenant's story and bade him escort them to his stockade.

Here the Spaniards expressed surprise that there were only five men in the party and that they had come so far without horses. Pike replied that his expedition consisted of several parties—not thinking it "proper to give them any satisfaction." He reiterated his intention to descend the river and at the same time hinted that, if the governor at Santa Fé would send out an interpreter knowing French or English, he would be happy to describe in detail the motives of his expedition. This offer was well received, and next day the visitors left without informing the party that they were west of the Río Grande and in Spanish territory.

A few hours later four of Corporal Jackson's relief party, who had gone for the crippled soldiers, returned to report that of the three men found, only one could walk. He and the rest of the relief party were expected the following day. All three of the crippled soldiers, Jackson said, hailed their rescuers with "tears of joy." The two who had to be left behind took part of the bones from their frozen feet and sent them to their commander begging that they not be left to perish in the wilderness. "Ah! little did they know my heart; if they could suspect me of conduct so ungenerous," Pike remarked.

Those men not reached by the relief party were over 180 miles distant, and their rescue would be difficult. For this undertaking two of the strongest men at the stockade volunteered on February 19. They planned to recross the mountains and use, if they could, the horses abandoned near the camp on the Arkansas, where the first men had been left.

Meanwhile, Pike and the others remained at the stockade, certain that more Spanish visitors would soon appear. They had not long to wait, for on February 26 one hundred Spanish dragoons and mounted militia were sighted approaching from the east. While the main body halted about fifty yards from the stockade, Pike invited their two officers to come in. This act elicited a cordial response and a present of food, which the officers brought from their own supplies.

As neither the Americans nor the Spaniards had breakfasted, Pike and his two guests sat down together. The Spanish commander—Lieutenant Ignacio Saltelo, Pike called him —speaking through his French interpreter, explained that the governor of New Mexico had heard that Pike was lost and now offered his assistance in guiding him and his men to the Red River, a journey of eight days east from Santa Fé.

"What! Is this not the Red River?" Pike asked in surprise. When Saltelo responded that it was the Río Grande, the Lieutenant appeared yet more bewildered than before. He at once ordered a soldier to take down the American flag and put it away, reasoning that the Spaniards "must have positive orders to take me in."

Was Pike sincere in believing that he was west of the Red River and not the Río Grande, or was his behavior before the Spaniards mere pretense? The answer would unlock much of the mystery of his journey. He himself steadfastly denied the charge that he knew he was in Spanish territory. Yet there is evidence to the contrary, and it is hard to believe that his surprise was genuine when he learned the true location of his Río Conejos camp.

141

Lieutenant Saltelo now tactfully suggested that Pike visit the governor at Santa Fé. "His mildness induced me to tell him that I would march," Pike wrote. But he informed the Spanish officer that he intended to leave two men at the stockade to receive the soldiers who were yet to return from the mountains, explaining that they would never come to Santa Fé without being ordered. To this Saltelo raised no objection.

When the troops outside learned of the American's willingness to go to Santa Fé, their pleasure was apparent: they had expected a fight. However, Pike's men were dubious about the journey, openly expressing belief that the Spaniards were not to be trusted.

Both parties prepared to march next day, February 27. Pike was disconcerted to learn that Lieutenant Saltelo and half the troops would remain behind until his six men still in the mountains had returned. But he was in no position to resist, for it was becoming apparent that the governor had ordered, not invited, him to Santa Fé.

With two of his men left behind at the stockade, Pike and five soldiers departed with the other half of the Spanish force. At least the Americans were supplied with horses for their journey; they would not have to walk. Their route lay almost due south about ten miles east of the Río Grande and parallel to it. Almost at once they felt a change in the climate: the snow had melted on the plains, and "vegetation was sprouting."

Of the several Pueblo villages, one of particular interest to the Americans was the mission settlement of San Juan, where lived the "president priest of the province." It was completely enclosed by a mud wall and had a population of about one thousand Spanish subjects. At the gates the travelers were met by a great crowd of the inhabitants, mostly Indians. The presence of the strangers obviously caused much excitement among the natives, several dozen old men and children following them and their escort down the narrow streets toward the center of the town. Others gathered on the flat roofs and in the doorways to watch the procession on its way to the home of the priest.

When they arrived at the clergyman's door, all the men dismounted, while the priest welcomed the American lieutenant, and invited him in for food and drink. Pike's men were led to rooms in the same building. This hospitality and comfort must have been a welcome change.

Pike sat with the priest for several hours, enjoying such luxuries as coffee, chocolate, wines, and various dishes, well seasoned and very tasty. Afterward, as he prepared to enter the room in which his men were quartered, he was addressed in broken English by a stranger who was standing near by. This person, a Frenchman, claimed he had been a prisoner of the Spaniards for three years and could not get out of the country. He began posthaste to ply the Lieutenant with questions above his entrance into Spanish territory and the motives of his journey.

Perceiving that the fellow was a spy, Pike had his men seize him and threatened to chastize him unless he confessed his real purpose in coming to their quarters. The man proved to be none other than Baptiste La Lande, the same La Lande against whom Pike had received the claims of William Morrison. He complained bitterly of his ill treatment by the Spaniards, who, he said, had taken his goods and would not let him return to the States.

"After this confession," Pike recorded, "I ordered my men to release him, and told him that I looked upon him as too contemptible for further notice; but that he might tell the governor, the next time he employed emissaries, to choose

143

those of more ability and sense; and that I questioned if his Excellency would find the sifting of us an easy task." Without further conversation, La Lande took his leave and went directly to the priest. There he reported, as was later learned, that the American lieutenant was a former governor of Illinois Territory, and this statement, which Pike would neither confirm nor deny, added measurably to his prestige among the Spaniards.

The next day, Pike, again entertained by the priest, partook too freely of the father's wine, became tipsy, and afterward resolved to be more abstemious in the future. His host proved as voluble as the wine was potent. Despite his years of isolation, he had a remarkable interest in natural history and was master of several languages.

However when Pike demonstrated some of his astronomical instruments, he found that his host was almost wholly ignorant of mathematics. Inquiry brought the revelation, said Pike, that Spain took care to prevent any study of science by her subjects in the new world, so that they could not compare the local scene with that of any other country. Pike observed that the priest and those inhabitants who were allowed to look through his telescope were much more impressed than any of the uncivilized Indians he had visited.

From San Juan the party proceeded to Santa Cruz, a village of some two thousand inhabitants six miles to the south, a short distance from Santa Fé, the provincial capital of New Mexico. As they approached it, Pike was reminded of the flatboats he had seen poling their way down the Ohio in the spring, for from a distance the adobe houses resembled a fleet of such craft. The domes of the local church towered up in majestic contrast.

Here, riding through the streets, they attracted the same

View of early Santa Fé and vicinity
from the east

crowd of curious onlookers as before. Pike and his six men suggested savages from a strange land, with their long beards, haggard faces, and shaggy hair; few had shoes, and none possessed a hat. So miserable did they appear that the inhabitants of Santa Fé, mostly civilized Indians, later inquired of them whether they lived in houses or in camps like the Indians, and whether the people of their country wore hats.

Pike was humiliated at his sorry figure. "When we presented ourselves at Santa Fe I was dressed in a pair of blue trousers, mockinsons, blanket coat, and a cap made of scarlet cloth lined with fox skin; my poor fellows were in leggins, breech cloths and leather coats." They must at least have been picturesque.

Santa Fé, one of the earliest Spanish settlements in the Southwest, had been settled, according to local tradition, around 1583. Pike estimated its population in 1807 at about five thousand.[1] It was at the foot of the Sangre de Cristo Range, 25 miles east of the Río Grande, and 550 miles up the Chihuahua Trail from Chihuahua. For several centuries trading caravans had plied this trail, the round trip requiring almost five months.

Years before the Spaniards settled the province of New Mexico, they had shown an unusual interest in the region because of the tales of the wealth which it was supposed to possess. And late in the sixteenth century the King of Spain ordered that the northern lands be added to the empire. The task was completed eventually, and Santa Fé was made the capital. It soon became the center of a great mission field, of trade, and of agriculture. At least half its population in 1807 were Spanish soldiers, traders, and churchmen.

[1] The official Mexican census for Santa Fé in 1827 put the population at 5,160.

Pike observed that corn, wheat, rye, barley, rice, and tobacco were grown throughout the region surrounding Santa Fé. Considering it more honorable to be agriculturists than mechanics, the Spaniards left manufacturing to the civilized Indians. The natives were skilled and industrious artisans, and made vast quantities of pottery, blankets of superior quality, cigars, and cotton, woolen, and leather goods which were carried to Mexico in ever increasing amounts.

Josiah Gregg in *Commerce of the Prairies* described Santa Fé some three decades after Pike's visit: "The town is very irregularly laid out, and most of the streets are little better than common highways traversing scattered settlements which are interspersed with cornfields nearly sufficient to supply the inhabitants with grain.

"The only attempt at anything like architectural compactness and procession consists in four tiers of every possible description. They stand around the public square, and comprise the Palicio, or Governor's house, the Custom house, the Barracks (with which is connected the fearful calabozo), the Casa consistorial of the Alcaldes, the Capilla de los Soldaros, or Military Chapel, besides several private residences, as well as most of the shops of the American traders."

Pike described the town as situated on a large creek and laid out in an oblong square, covering about a mile from east to west. Its houses, mostly one-story adobe, flat-roofed, and rather ugly outside, were sometimes richly furnished inside. A few had windows with glass panes, and almost every residence had a thatched awning across the front to shade its brick-paved entrance. These street-level entrances, extending from one house to another, served passers-by for a sidewalk.

By the time the procession reached the Palace square, quite a crowd had gathered. Halting at Governor Alancaster's door, the party all dismounted, and Lieutenant Pike was escorted inside. After a brief wait in the Governor's anteroom, Pike was admitted to his inner chamber and very courteously greeted. Alancaster first wanted to know why he was in Spanish territory and how many men he had.

Informed that the party consisted of fifteen men, he asked if this included Dr. Robinson. Pike now made his first tactical error by answering, "No," for Robinson had already informed the Governor that he was part of the American expedition, and Alancaster's suspicion of his "prisoner" was thus confirmed.

This incident is another link in the chain of evidence cited to prove that Pike was a spy. Pike, obviously not a practiced liar, later explained that he knew Robinson to be a prisoner at that time and was concerned for his safety should America and Spain be already at war, for Robinson might then, under the rules of war, be executed as a spy.

Alancaster now sent Pike to his quarters, with orders to return with his papers at seven that evening. At that time Pike was surprised to find a fellow countryman enlisted as interpreter. This was Solomon Colley, formerly a sergeant in the American Army and more recently one of the famous Philip Nolan expedition of 1800.

Nolan was the first American to make a visible splash in the sea of Texas history. As early as 1785 he seems to have been engaged in illegal trade between the United States and this Spanish province. Later (in 1801) he was ambushed and killed by a Spanish force near present Waco, Texas. Nine of his men were then taken to Mexico and obliged to roll dice to determine their fate: one to be hanged and the others to be held in bondage for life. One who eventually escaped, Peter Ellis Bean, had a subsequent career notable in the history of Texas.

Pike's discovery of one of Nolan's party at Santa Fé, and also of others in the interior of Mexico, refutes the common belief that none of the prisoners but Bean was ever heard from again. Pike exerted every effort in behalf of these miserable survivors, but if he did any good, the record has not survived.

Since leaving his Río Conejos camp, the Lieutenant had jealously guarded his personal papers, distributing some of the more important of them among his men, who concealed them under their clothing. The rest were in Pike's trunk. When he was ordered to show Alancaster these papers, Pike brought only those then in his trunk, but the Governor did not seem particularly interested in examining them. Secure now in the belief that little more would be said to him, Pike was disturbed to learn, on going to his quarters, that the townspeople were plying his men with liquor. He therefore took from them all his documents and put them in the trunk, only to have it seized at once by Spanish soldiers. He had been tricked.

Once in Alancaster's hands, these papers were enough to convince the Governor that Pike had ulterior motives. Therefore, the Americans were to be sent to Chihuahua for questioning by higher officials.

On hearing this decision, Pike demanded whether his party were to be treated as prisoners or as volunteers. Alancaster's reply, though vague enough, left little doubt in Pike's mind of his true status. He did not think, he then replied, that his expedition was a greater infringement upon Spanish territory than that of Malgares into Louisiana in the previous year. "I do not understand," replied Alancaster, and with that the conference ended.

Again in his quarters, Pike prepared a letter to the Governor officially protesting his treatment as a common spy. To his sergeant, in charge of the other members of the party who had not yet arrived at Santa Fé, he wrote, "Keep up the good discipline and do not be alarmed or discouraged." On the eve of departure he had a final call from Alancaster, extremely courteous as usual, who gave him a new shirt and other clothing from his personal wardrobe.

At noon on March 4, the seven Americans, with several Spanish troops, joined a caravan of civilians and traders departing for Chihuahua. Pike and his men were allowed to keep their side arms, but the Lieutenant was ordered not to take any notes on the country through which he was to travel.

The caravan moved slowly southward, everyone mounted and the supplies carried by pack horses. A number of Pueblo villages, like those of San Juan and Santa Fé, lay along the way. At each stop Pike was quartered with the resident priest where he could enjoy the wine and conversation of these generous hosts. Had Pike been a Roman Catholic, he doubtless would have fared even better. Several of the priests indeed tried to convert him, but without success.

At Albuquerque, on the east bank of the Río Grande, Pike observed the great activities of the natives, digging canals to lead the waters of the river to the plains. It reminded him, he wrote, of his boyhood, when he used to read of the canals in Egypt and pictured them much as the ones he now observed.

While the caravan and troops rested at Albuquerque, Pike, with a small escort of Spanish soldiers, visited the commandant of the region, who lived in a little village across the river. When he entered the quarters, a pleasant surprise awaited him. "I saw a man sitting by the fire reading a book; with blooming cheeks, fine complexion, and a genius-speaking eye. . . . It was Robinson!"

Overjoyed by their reunion, both tried to talk at once. Robinson said he was still a political prisoner but nonetheless was allowed to practice his profession. He was glad of the opportunity of "examining the manners and customs of the people, to endeavor to ascertain their political and religious feelings, and to gain every other species of information which would be necessary to our country and ourselves."

Apparently, then, the motives of Pike's expedition were more than the mere acquiring of geographic and scientific knowledge.

Dr. Robinson now joined his former comrades on their journey. From Albuquerque they were under the command of the genial Lieutenant Malgares, the same who had gone into Louisiana in search of Pike the year before. The two officers soon became close friends.

The rest of the journey was far from the monotonous march Pike had anticipated. At frequent stops from village to village, Malgares allowed him complete freedom in conversing with the people and recording his observations. Pike found the Spanish subjects possessed "heaven-like qualities of hospitality and kindness." The Americans were entertained frequently by town officials at banquets and balls, with always a "handsome display of beauty." Usually the prettiest girls of a region were assembled before the caravan arrived. A round of feasting, cock fights, dancing, and merry-making would be the order of the day.

Pike often mentioned in his journal the women of New Spain, but there is no evidence that his contact with them was anything but that of an interested observer. He found them mostly brunette, with very dark hair and eyes and with fine teeth. "Finding that the men only regard them as objects of gratification to the sensual passions, they have lost every idea of that feast of reason and flow of soul which arises from the intercourse of two refined and virtuous minds." The Lieutenant sadly concluded that the Spaniards gave their horses as much concern as their women—the status of the latter being not unlike that of the inmates of a Turkish harem.

On March 21, the caravan reached the halfway mark on the journey from Santa Fé to Chihuahua when they sighted the cross-roads of the continent, El Paso del Norte. This settlement occupied the spot where the Río Grande del Norte cuts through the mountains and emerges on the plains. The lower part of the stream was long called by the Spaniards the Río Bravo, the name "Río Grande del Norte" being reserved for its upper portions. Today it all bears a single name, and from Colorado to the Gulf is called the Río Grande.

El Paso del Norte of 1807 was on the south bank, and the site of the present El Paso, then vacant, was not occupied until many years later. Cabeza de Vaca was here in 1536, but permanent settlement dates only from around 1659. Pike found the region one of the most flourishing he had seen outside the United States. Some of the large ranches boasted upwards of twenty thousand sheep and one thousand head of cattle.

The party had three pleasant days at El Paso before pushing on again. Lieutenant Malgares took Pike on a round of the local gambling houses, and seems to have won large sums. Pike either did not play, or did not confess so much to his journal.

Here, too, he met, for the first time, members of the Apache nation. "These people appeared to be perfectly independent in their manner and were the only savages I saw in the Spanish dominions whose spirits were not humbled—whose necks were not bowed to the yoke of their invaders."

151

On being told of their valor and cunning, he was glad he had not come upon them with just his little party out on the plains.

The march on to Chihuahua, a distance of some 230 miles, was uneventful. It was accomplished in only nine days, for the settlements here, and consequently the stops, were fewer.

Chihuahua, with about seven thousand inhabitants, was the capital of the Biscay Province and was, compared to other towns visited along the way, a truly magnificent place. Its public buildings revealed greater elegance of taste, while some domestic structures, though of one story, were cornered and faced with stone. However, the streets of Chihuahua, like those of Santa Fé, were just as nature left them save for a few roughly paved sidewalks.

General Don Nimesio Salcedo, who had been the last Spanish governor of Louisiana, was now governor of Biscay. Pike found him to be a man of middle age, fifty-five perhaps, who greeted his guest sternly and yet graciously. "You have given us and yourself a great deal of trouble." "On my part entirely unsought," Pike responded, "and on that of the Spanish government voluntary."

Each document in Pike's trunk now had to be scrutinized, Pike explaining the nature of his papers as best he could. Salcedo decided to have them all translated so that he could study them more thoroughly. Pike, however, was allowed to keep those he said were personal. He was not to discuss politics or religion in Chihuahua, but otherwise, the Governor announced, he could do as he wished until they had further need of him.

He was quartered in the home of a man named Walker, a former American officer then in the service of Spain, and was indeed well treated, a frequent guest of prominent officials, even of Governor Salcedo. However, he soon realized that "in this city the proverb was literally true that the walls have ears; for scarcely anything could pass that his Excellency did not know it in a few hours." Yet Pike was not unhappy in his new surroundings.

Two members of the ill-fated Nolan expedition were living in Chihuahua. One, an old Negro, formerly a slave of one of Nolan's followers, was now employed by Walker. The other, David Ferro, formerly of New York, had served in the Third Sub-Legion in 1794 under Captain Zebulon Pike, the Lieutenant's father. Now a prisoner of the Spaniards, he begged Pike with tears to intercede in his behalf, and the Lieutenant was deeply moved by his plea.

While Pike was enjoying the hospitality of the town, Salcedo was having his papers translated. Their contents persuaded him that Pike's expedition had ulterior motives, but he hesitated to do anything that might provoke retaliation from Washington. He therefore decided to return the Americans to their country with a strongly worded protest to certain officials of the United States government.

One of these officials was General James Wilkinson. To him, Salcedo now wrote in part: "Your excellency is not ignorant of the repeated representations made by the king's minister in the United States, and by the Marquis of Cassa Calvo while he was in Louisiana, summoning [admonishing] the American government to carry into effect any projects of extending its expeditions into territories unquestionably belonging to his Majesty. You must therefore, without any further observations or remarks on my part, be satisfied that the documents contain evident, unequivocal proofs that an offense of magnitude has been committed against his Majesty, and that every individual of this party ought to have been considered as prisoners on the very spot.

"Notwithstanding such substantial and well grounded motives as would have warranted such a measure, also wishing to give the widest latitude to the subsisting system of harmony and good understanding, and above all, being finally persuaded that your Excellency would take such steps as your judgment might suggest as best calculated to prevent any bad consequences on the occasion, I have concluded to keep in this general government all the papers presented by Lieutenant Pike, and to give him and his men full liberty to return to Your Excellency, after having treated them with attention, and offered them every assistance they stood in need of."[2]

Before Pike began his return journey, Salcedo advanced him one thousand dollars to defray the expenses of his party while they were in Spanish territory; and further sums were lent him before he reached Louisiana. These were later repaid by the government.[3]

Salcedo also reported on the Pike expedition to the foreign office in Madrid. He thought the American lieutenant was a spy and feared that Alancaster had made a grave error in sending him to Chihuahua, affording him opportunity to view further the state of Spain's preparedness. (Alancaster was shortly replaced.)

The Spanish chargé d' affaires at Washington, Valentin de Foronda, later addressed a letter to Secretary of State Madison in which he made this significant comment relative to Pike's arrest: "According to the law of nations Dr. Robinson and the officer Pike should have been treated as spies;

[2] Salcedo to Wilkinson, April 8, 1807, printed in Coues, *op. cit.*, 815–17.

[3] In addition to the money advanced to Pike in 1807, the Spanish government later filed claims totaling more than $22,000 which they reported had been expended in searching for Pike's party, as well as for other government-sponsored expeditions into "Spanish Territory." Jefferson refused to meet the exorbitant Spanish demands.

They were apprehended in a country concerning which there was not the least dispute, the least doubt, but that it belonged to my August Sovereign. It is true that the officer alleged that he lost his way. The statement may be true, but it may also be a pretext, and the latter is more probable. You know that if such excuses are satisfactory a spy could never be condemned."[4]

Madison informed Foronda that "this government never employed a spy for any purpose"; and that Pike's mission was to ascend the Arkansas and descend the Red, to ascertain their geography. But the Spaniards were not satisfied with this explanation, and, what with one thing and another, the two countries finally broke off diplomatic relations.

The twenty-one documents taken from Pike remained in Mexico for over a century. Nineteen of them were found there by an American scholar in 1907 and were returned to the United States three years later. Historians had long supposed that they would contain the key to Pike's guilt or innocence, but the story of their discovery and return proved to be more interesting than their contents.

Pike's route to San Antonio lay due east along the old Chihuahua-Coahuila Trail. Lieutenant Malgares, still acting as escort, now told him that he could make no further notes about the country through which they traveled. "At first I felt considerably indignant, and was on the point of refusing to comply, but thinking for a moment of the many politenesses I had received from his hands induced me merely to bow assent with a smile. We proceeded on our route, but had not gone far before I made a pretext to halt, established my boy as a vedet [guard], sat down peaceably under a brush and made my

---

[4] Valentin de Foronda to James Madison, August 22, 1807, as quoted in Cox, *The Early Exploration of Louisiana*, 137.

notes. This course I pursued ever after, not without some considerable degree of trouble to separate myself from the party."

To conceal these notes, Pike hid them in his men's rifle barrels. Despite the loss of his twenty-one documents, which actually contained little pertinent information, he managed to collect an incredible amount of data relative to Mexico. His subsequent reports to General Wilkinson and to the federal government contain a detailed exposition of the manners, morals, politics, and religion of the people. His further data on the natural resources, population, government, geography, and military installation of the country make up the first adequate report on the Spanish provinces in North America brought back by an American traveler.

Pike's conduct while a "prisoner" of the Spaniards seems commendable, whatever his motives in permitting his own capture. His behavior and remarks reflect a keen intellect, and his manner won friends among his adversaries.

On June 1, 1807, Lieutenant Pike, Dr. Robinson, and the six American soldiers, with the Spanish troops under Malgares, reached the south bank of the Río Grande and stopped at the frontier village of Presidio del Río Grande, about forty miles below present-day Eagle Pass, Texas. As usual, the natives and officials were cordial, and the party was taken that evening to see a troupe of acrobats. "They were in no wise extraordinary in their performances except in language, which would bring a blush on the cheek of the most abandoned of the female sex in the United States."

Resuming their march next evening, the travelers reached San Antonio after six days of constant riding. Pike's observations of the Texas province were not more modest than those of a typical Texan today: "It has one of the most delightful temperatures in the world. . . . Take it generally, it is one of the richest, most prolific, and best watered countries in North America."

As for the people: "Their general subjects of conversation are women, money, and horses, which appear to be the only objects, in their estimate, worthy of consideration. . . . Their games are cards, billiards, horse-racing, and cock fighting, the first and last of which are carried to the most extravagant lengths, losing, and winning immense sums." In some respects the place has changed but little since.

From San Antonio to Natchitoches, Louisiana, the journey required a little more than two weeks, the party arriving at 4 p.m., July 1, 1807, after a year's absence from the States.[5] Pike's final entry reads: "Language cannot express the gaiety of my heart when I once beheld the standards of my country waved aloft. 'All Hail!' cried I, the ever sacred name of the country, in which is embraced that of kindred, friends, and every other tie which is dear to the soul of man!"

[5] The eight members of the Pike expedition who were left at the stockade or in the Colorado mountains did not get home until about a year later. Their adventures are discussed later.

157

12

"*You Must Be Cautious*"

A great wave of excitement swept the country in the wake of Burr's arrest for treason in January, 1807. Almost everyone believed him guilty, and many wished to see him hanged. Moreover, there were some men in Washington and New Orleans who particularly hoped for quick conviction. Among these were Thomas Jefferson and James Wilkinson.

By the time the trial opened, General Wilkinson had become for most citizens the hero of the hour and the savior of his country. But in New Orleans, where he had spent so many years in dubious intrigues, there were still many persons who were cold to the General's glory. They remembered his reputation and resented his declaring martial law and arresting all who questioned his motives. Some were even persuaded that he was himself involved in Burr's conspiracy.

Burr came to trial in the Federal Circuit Court at Richmond, Virginia, on May 22, 1807. Wilkinson, the principal witness against him, had promised to bring "undoubted proof of Burr's guilt," but he failed to arrive until several weeks after the trial had opened, for he had been "suppressing the still surviving conspiracy" in New Orleans.

It was while thus engaged that he had word of Pike's arrival in Chihuahua, and of the latter's intention to return to Natchitoches. He now addressed a letter to Captain Pike at Natchitoches (for Pike's promotion had become effective in August, 1806, during his absence in the West).

Wilkinson's epistle is extremely interesting, in view of the belief that there were ulterior motives in his authorizing Pike's southwestern journey. He first expressed a happy surprise in learning that his protégé was still alive when he had thought him dead. "Let it suffice for me to say to you," he then continued, "that you must be cautious, extremely cautious, how you breathe a word; because publicity may excite a spirit of adventure adverse to the interest of our government, or injurious to the maturity of those plans which may hereafter be found necessary and justifiable by the government."[1]

This statement may be additional evidence of Wilkinson's involvement in the Burr conspiracy. Apparently the General was afraid that Pike's actions might be harmful to both himself and Pike, hence this warning to be cautious. We cannot doubt that Wilkinson was capable of treason, and it seems clear that Pike's Arkansas journey in some way fitted into Wilkinson's personal plans, and probably into those of Aaron Burr. How much, then, we may ask, did Pike himself know of Wilkinson's true purpose?

It will be recalled that in Wilkinson's written instructions prior to the Arkansas expedition in 1806, he had cautioned Pike to be discreet and to prevent alarm by the Spaniards should he "fall in with any of their parties while in the vicinity of Santa Fe." He further warned his subordinate that he would be held responsible for consequences.

"Should I encounter a party from the villages near Santa Fe," Pike had replied, "I have thought it would be a good

[1] Wilkinson to Pike, New Orleans, May 20, 1807, War Records Division, National Archives, Washington, D. C.

policy to give them to understand that we were about to join our troops near Natchitoches, but had been uncertain about the headwaters of the rivers over which we had passed; but that now, if the commandant approved of it, we may pay him a visit of politeness."[2] This statement appears innocent enough had not Pike later often asserted that he had no intention of approaching Santa Fé.

Further evidence suggests that Pike's role in the Southwest was more than that of explorer. On October 2, 1806, while encamped near the Pawnee village on the Republican River, he observed in a letter to Wilkinson: "Any number of men who may reasonably be calculated on would find no difficulty in marching by the route we came, with baggage wagons, field artillery, and all the usual appendages of a small army; and if all the route to Santa Fe should be of the same description, in case of war I would pledge my life and what is infinitely dearer, my honor, for the successful march of a reasonable body of troops into the province of New Mexico."[3]

On the basis of this and similar statements, Kyle S. Crichton bluntly calls Pike a traitor and finds him at best "highly unethical and untruthful."[4] He contends that the Lieutenant's behavior—in the face of denials that he had any idea of getting near Santa Fé—was rather odd in one who claimed to be a loyal American officer.

Indeed, the evidence most damaging to Pike's reputation

[2] Pike to Wilkinson, Village De Charette, July 22, 1806, War Records Division, National Archives.

[3] This letter is now in the War Records Division, National Archives. It was among the twenty-one documents taken from Pike by the Spaniards (and later returned to the United States in 1910). Its contents, more than anything else, convinced the Spaniards that Pike was a spy.

[4] Kyle S. Crichton, "Zeb Pike," *Scribner's Magazine*, Vol. LXXXII (1927), 462–67. Crichton goes further than any other writer in condemning Pike, but he fails to take account of much of the evidence in Pike's favor.

probably lies in the location of his camp on the Río Conejos, obviously in Spanish territory. His champions have for the most part been hard pressed to explain this action, but Hart and Hulbert manage it rather simply: they maintain, as has been related, that the choice of this particular camp site is of no significance—that Pike marked the Río Grande as the "Red River" and had no chance to correct his maps before they were taken from him.

"If it was the Rio Grande," these editors continue, "our claims extended to it, including the right of navigation. And surely the fiercest Spanish partisan would not have gainsaid the party's right under international law, to save their lives by going where firewood could be secured. If it was the Red River, as Pike's recovered maps still prove he thought it was, the American claim was as good on one side or the other."[5] Like so much of the evidence for and against Pike, this argument is plausible and yet inconclusive. Passing over the question of his choice of a camp site, there is yet reason to believe that Pike was not displeased at his capture and detention by the Spaniards.

In his further defense, Hart and Hulbert argue that if the southwestern trip had been to spy out the land for Aaron Burr, Pike would not have been chosen to command it. Other men, with a real knowledge of New Mexico and the Spanish language, were available; and one of these, going as a trader, would not have attracted the attention and suspicion aroused by a troop of armed horsemen. "More than that, if Wilkinson and Burr had seriously wanted a reconnaissance of New Mexico, they would have wanted it in 1805—not 1806 or 1807. A serious reconnaissance of New Mexico required an accurate military strategist. . . . Only an expert, supplied with the

[5] Hart and Hulbert, *op. cit.*, *xcii.*

best instruments and the best methods of transporting them, could have fixed altitude, latitude, and longitude correctly." Both the validity and fallacy of this assertion are too evident to need comment.

Pike emphatically denied receiving any secret instructions from Wilkinson in any way connecting his activity with the designs of Burr; and in view of his character and services it is hard to question his sincerity. This, of course, does not acquit Wilkinson, Pike's staunch friend, of the charges of complicity with Burr. A man of Wilkinson's hankering for power and wealth, his record as a pensioner of the Spanish, and his notorious cleverness, would naturally be suspected of personal motives in authorizing the Arkansas or any other expedition. James Riley Jacobs calls him "the most voluble and egotistical high ranking officer in the history of the United States army— a political opportunist with a military sheen."

Long before Pike had returned from Mexico and before the Burr trial had begun, there were rumors afoot that the young explorer was implicated in the Wilkinson-Burr affair, and these could not fail to reach the ears of his family.

On July 15, 1807, his father, Major Zebulon Pike, wrote from Lawrenceburg, Indiana to General Dearborn, the secretary of war: "Permit me to request the Honor of a few lines informing if Z. M. Pike received orders from His Government on His late exploring expedition, from the President, Yourself, or Genl. Wilkinson, and if any or how late the last information or communications from Him. I need not mention how disagreeable a state of Suspense is, nor, to move your sympathy, to say more than that the anxiety and concern, exhibited for His safety, by an affectionate Mother and Wife, is Great. By way of consolation to the former, I have thought proper to extend the probable Period of His return, untill this month;

Mrs. Pike is now beginning to lose confidence in my opinion, consequently my consolating influence is daily lesening, and Her afflictions increasing."[6]

Major Pike's letter, now on file in the War Records Department of the National Archives, is endorsed in General Dearborn's handwriting: "Tell him his son is safe, and is probably at Natchitoches." Dearborn's failure to account for Pike's authorization may indicate that he, too, had some apprehension about the true purposes of the Arkansas expedition.

It may be recalled that when Wilkinson ordered Pike into the Southwest, war was imminent between the United States and Spain. As commander-in-chief of the army in the West, Wilkinson is not to be condemned for trying to get information about a likely foe. So Pike may well have reasoned that the data Wilkinson wanted was to be used for a legitimate purpose, national defense. Always a loyal officer, he was not one to question his commander's motives.

Soon after his return to the States, Captain Pike set about editing for publication his journal and papers. That they were actually published three years later should of itself lessen the suspicion of Pike's good faith. Moreover, the reader of his narrative cannot fail to admire his spirit and the devotion he inspired in his men. Not only is the journal a worthy contribution to Americana, but it contains a record of human daring, hardship, devotion, and achievement seldom equalled.

Perhaps Pike's relation to Wilkinson and the Burr conspiracy is best indicated in a document used as evidence against Wilkinson at the trial of Burr. Judge Timothy Kibby of the District of St. Charles in Upper Louisiana had affixed his signature to an affidavit on July 6, 1807, reading in part as fol-

[6] Major Pike's letter to the Secretary of War is reprinted in Coues, *op. cit.*, *xxi.*

lows: "I asked the Genl. if Mr. Pike was sent by the Government of the United States. He replied no that it was his own (the Genl's.) plan and if Mr. Pike suckseeded he the Genl. would be placed out of reach of his enemies and that in the course of eighteen months he would be in a situation (if the plan suckseeded) to call his Damn foes to an a/c for their Deeds. I asked the Genl. if he did not apprehend danger from the Spaniards, knowing their jealous disposition, on Mr. Pike's account with a party of American soldiers at Santa fee. he answered that Mr. Pike and his party would have documents to shew which would make them as safe as in Philadelphia."[7]

We may conclude from the brevity of notices about it in western newspapers that Captain Pike's Arkansas journey actually excited little public attention. Moreover, the press was then very busy with the dramatic events at Richmond. On August 29, 1807, the *National Intelligencer*, an outstanding paper of the day, carried only this short entry: "Captain Pike, who has been detained in the interior provinces of Spanish America, arrived at this place [Natchitoches] in the evening of 30th last month."

John Sibley, previously mentioned, gave a brief account of the Pike expedition in a letter to his son, Samuel Hopkins Sibley, dated June 20, 1807: "Captain Pike, Doctor Robinson & Party arrived here [Natchitoches] this day [Pike states that it was July 1, the following day] from the interior of New Spain, last fall they were Sent up Missouri, ordered to cross over the heads of Arkensa & Red Rivers & Descend the latter, they were at the source of the Arkansa from thence fall upon some of the Waters of River Grand in the Vicinity of

---

[7] See "Papers of Zebulon Montgomery Pike," *American Historical Review*, Vol. XIII, No. 4 (1908), 798–827, for the full text of Kibby's affidavit and a summary of the reasons for suspecting Pike and Wilkinson of complicity.

Sta Fee the capital of New Mexico. They were taken by the Spaniards, & six months elapsed before it was known what had become of them, at length we heard of them in the Spanish Interior Provinces, they were conducted by armed men from Province to Province, till they arrived, here, their Instruments and Papers they were permitted to retain and no doubt have made important discoveries. I have seen them only a few Minutes."

Neither of these accounts of Pike's return reflect suspicion that his journey had been connected with the Burr conspiracy. But if we may judge from the Captain's behavior, he was subject to considerable criticism and the motives of his expedition were generally suspected. Characteristically, he dispatched at once a letter to the Secretary of War, demanding his exoneration.

"I can with pleasure observe," replied General Dearborn, "that although the two exploring expeditions were not previously ordered by the President of the United States, there were frequent communications on the subject of each between General Wilkinson and this department of which the President of the United States was from time to time acquainted." Dearborn closed with an assurance that Pike's services were held in high esteem by the President, and that he personally considered the public much indebted to him for the way he had performed his duties.[8]

Such a statement from the Secretary of War must have been gratifying to Pike, who now felt that the purity of his motives had been vindicated. Copies were sent to Congress and published in newspapers with the result that popular sentiment against Pike dwindled away except around New Or-

[8] Dearborn to Pike, Washington, D. C., February 24, 1808, War Records Division, National Archives.

leans and Natchez. There a few editors continued the assault, calling Pike "the beast of Santa Fé" and "a parasite of Wilkinson." This was the price Pike had to pay for his steadfast loyalty to a man now thoroughly discredited and branded "a second Benedict Arnold."

Typical of these attacks was an article of July 27, 1809, in the Natchez *Weekly Chronicle:* "A striking coincidence of opinion prevails among all parties in the United States relative to Wilkinson. Here where his atrocities were first ushered into light, and where the effects of them are still palpable and present, there are some who were concerned with—and others who were his dupes, who pretend not to credit the charges which have been exhibited against him. It can only be a pretense—a person might as well deny the light of the sun, as to deny the truths which are well known."

A few weeks later the same paper accused Pike of having once "beaten and bullied" the editor of the Reading (Pennsylvania) *Eagle,* because "he had the impudence to deny the infallibility of John Adams." And again on March 5, 1810, it editorialized: "Those who advocate Wilkinson either know nothing of the man or are his minors."

Perhaps Pike received his most severe criticism in an unsigned letter to the editor of the New Orleans *Gazette,* in a December, 1809, issue: "I have seen a communication in the *Courier,* announcing the return of Captain D. Hughes, with the prisoners left by Major Pike [the promotion to major became effective May 3, 1808] in the Spanish provinces in the year 1807, with the exception of a Sergeant Meek, who was detained for having killed one of the party, who declared the purpose of Major Pike's journey was different from the one announced. I would like to know Messrs Printer if every man who suspects the object of the expedition not to be laudible or patriotic, is to be murdered? Is General Wilkinson and his myrmodors reduced to the alternative of putting to death the witness of their treachery? 'Dead men tell no tales' and perhaps the general might have escaped the justice of his country a little longer had he adopted the measures of Sergeant Meek for supressing evidence. But let the guilty tremble, whenever there is an investigation before Congress of the motives of Pike's expedition and the testimony then given will be of more consequence to the nation than the major's journal."

Although this story is quite interesting, its veracity is doubtful. The article cited in the *Courier* contains so garbled an account, with so many obvious errors, that its whole content must be questioned, including the charge that Meek killed one of the party to suppress unfavorable evidence.

In any case, the charge against Meek was really directed at Pike himself. Pike had learned of the alleged incident before returning to the States and in a letter written July 5, 1807, had mentioned it to Wilkinson. Governor Salcedo, he reported, had sent a dispatch to the governor of Texas, General Cordero, which arrived during the American's brief stop at San Antonio. In it Salcedo had erroneously charged that "the sergeant killed one of *his* men, in consequence of some improper conduct." The personal pronoun is here ambiguous, and it is not clear whether Salcedo had accused Meek of killing a Spaniard or an American.

One wonders how Pike, who had not been in direct communication with Meek's party, could so confidently deny the accusation. Salcedo's charge, on the other hand, may have been a mere pretense, to justify him should he hold the American prisoner to get more information from him.

As there was no Congressional investigation into the expedition (but only one to determine whether its members deserved double pay for their services, as with the Lewis-Clark journey), no official charges were brought against Pike or any of his men.[9]

A document now in the War Records Division of the National Archives, recorded May 3, 1808, and signed "Z. M. Pike, Captain," accounts for the entire eight members of the party left in Mexico. It states that the men had now returned to the United States and it lists them by name—including one William E. Meek, sergeant. Pike himself, already in Washington, appears to have assumed that all his men had by then reached Natchitoches.

Yet according to a story in the New Orleans *Courier* some months later, December 2, 1809, Pike's men did not return from Mexico until November 20, 1809. Seven of the eight, it said, were now back in the United States. Sergeant Meek had been retained by the Spaniards "for having nobly taken the life of one of his party, who attempted by an insinuation to inculpate the motives of the expedition to the heads of Red River and the frontier of New Spain." No further detail of Meek's fate has been recorded.

Across the void of almost a century and a half the legend of Pike's complicity with Wilkinson and Burr has persisted. The mystery of the contents of the papers taken from him by the Spaniards has helped to give the story life. So long as these documents remained unrecovered, many were certain that they could unlock the secret of Pike's collaboration and determine the degree of his guilt. Pike tried repeatedly to recover the

[9] Congress took the position that the tour was authorized by the commander of the United States Army. Therefore, its members merely acted in line of duty and were not entitled to extra compensation. In 1846, Pike's widow received $3,000 from the federal government because of her husband's three-year absence from his country while engaged in exploring the West.

papers down to the time of his death. Then within a few years they were forgotten.

Not until 1906 was there a serious effort to locate them and obtain their return to the United States. Colorado was then commemorating her centennial, and members of the State Memorial Association asked Congressman Franklin E. Brooks to obtain the Pike papers, if he could, for historical display during the celebration.

Scattered among the millions of documents in the National Archives are the letters which together tell the story of the quest for and the return of the Pike papers. First, Congressman Brooks asked Secretary of State Elihu Root, to inaugurate a search for the missing documents. Root passed on this project to the Embassy in Mexico City, and an investigation was begun at once. Officials of the Mexican national archives, unable to find any trace of the papers, suggested they had probably been sent to Spain, and might perhaps be found in the Archivo General de Indias at Seville.

A thorough search at Seville brought equally negative results—the papers could not be found. Could they have been transferred to the Spanish colonial archives at Havana? Here, too, the search proved fruitless. By now the Colorado celebration had run its course, and so the whole matter was dropped.

A few months later, however, in 1907, Secretary Root happened to go on an official mission to Mexico City. There he met an American scholar, Dr. Herbert E. Bolton, who was working in the national archives, and told him the story of his unsuccessful quest for Pike's papers. Professor Bolton promised to make a personal investigation. "I am glad to be able to inform you," he wrote a few weeks later, "that I have discovered the greater number of them—though not the most important ones, I fear—together with correspondence that explains their history since they were taken from Pike."[10]

Professor Bolton had, in fact, uncovered eighteen of the twenty-one documents, and a few days later he found yet another in a different section of the archives. The results of this discovery, with a reproduction of some of the more important items, appeared in the *American Historical Review* for July, 1908. Unfortunately, their contents revealed little that was not already known; and the two documents still missing continue to nourish the legend of Pike's complicity. Yet, after all, is it not absurd to suppose that Pike, assuming he wished to be captured, should have carried on his person evidence of his own treason?

The publication of the recovered papers caused a mild sensation in academic circles, but they were soon forgotten. In July, 1910, the nineteen items were returned to the United States through the collaboration of Enrique C. Creel, Mexican minister of foreign affairs and Henry Lane Wilson, United States ambassador to Mexico. They are now in the National Archives Building at Washington.

An examination of Pike's career makes it hard to believe that he could have plotted treason. His years of public service and personal sacrifice furnish convincing evidence to the contrary. His great fault apparently lies in an unflinching faith in Wilkinson. It is agreed that the feeblest insight must have perceived this man's double-dealing and that Pike was no dullard. Perhaps he was merely trying to justify, in his own eyes as in the eyes of others, the man who was his superior officer and his private patron. Pike seems to have been incapable of turning against a friend—in any circumstances.

[10] Herbert E. Bolton to Secretary Root, Mexico City, November 9, 1907, General Records of the Department of State, National Archives.

13

"The Salve of the Regiment"

GENERAL WILKINSON had ordered Pike, prior to his departure in 1806, to return to the United States via Natchitoches and thence to Washington. Pike had planned, therefore, to proceed from Natchitoches up the Mississippi, rejoin his family at Fort Bellefontaine, and then go by the Ohio to Pittsburgh and by land to Washington. However, when the explorer reached Louisiana in 1807, he found himself too weak to travel farther.

Meanwhile, Mrs. Pike, on learning of her husband's expected return to Natchitoches, had departed for that city with her little daughter. Pike does not relate the circumstances of the family reunion, but one can imagine that it was a happy one, even though marred by tragic news, for the father was now to learn of the birth and death of a son.[1]

Before going on to Washington, Captain Pike had a number of pressing duties to perform. There were many letters to write—letters to his parents, friends, the War Department, General Wilkinson, General Salcedo in Mexico, and others. He had to make official reports of the expedition, perfect his maps and charts, and arrange and edit his journal. Despite ill-

---

[1] This child, one of four Pike children to die in infancy, was buried at Bellefontaine.

ness and bad eyesight, which prevented his working more than an hour a day, Pike eventually disposed of his labors and prepared for the long trip to Washington.

His personal letters after 1807 indicate that his personality had changed since he was a young lieutenant yet unknown to fame. Two years of travel, with countless hardships and grave responsibilities, had matured him far beyond his twenty-seven years. Frequently, the lives of his men and the welfare of his country had rested upon his personal decisions. Never lacking in self-confidence, Pike now, more than ever, found a renewed faith in his own capacity. He felt sure he was destined for even greater undertakings.

Indeed, his fame soon spread throughout the world, and he seems to have reveled in the limelight. Not unmindful of his own greatness, he sometimes failed to resist the temptation to remind others of it. Yet he was also to discover that notoriety can be disconcerting. The continued attacks upon him because of his friendship for Wilkinson soon convinced the explorer that he was a victim of persecution. Doubtless his bitterness was aggravated by the sorrow of his son's death and a belief that neither he nor his father had been promoted as rapidly as their services had warranted.

"Colonel Butler's vacancy should have given me a captaincy," Pike wrote to his father, "nearly one year sooner than I obtained it. Many others have similar causes of complaint and should my country attempt to do us such injustice, may my right arm whether from my body if I would ever again extend it to save her from ruin and slavery—but take my family and retire to the haunts of the untutored savage—where if the heart is taught such revenge on the enemies of their tribes, it likewise dictates the protection of friends and justice to the merits of all. Where if the mind is not illuminated by the bright rays of science—the head is not filled with the craft, and the diplomatic deception of refined society."[2]

It was not long before further advancement soothed the wrath of the younger man, but for Major Zebulon Pike, his father, less could be expected. The old gentleman's memory had now grown so remarkably treacherous that it had become dangerous to assign him any important command. General Dearborn, however, generously allowed him to retire with the full pay and emoluments of a major. At the outbreak of the War of 1812, as has been related, he was made a colonel, his first promotion in twelve years, but in 1815 he was discharged as unfit for further service.

On September 19, 1807, Captain Pike, his wife Clara, and their four-year-old daughter Clarissa, boarded "one of the fastest vessels ever to sail from the port of New Orleans," and reached New York City about three weeks later. This metropolis already boasted 70,000 inhabitants and was second only to Philadelphia. In a few weeks they journeyed on to Washington by stage.

The federal capital in the last days of Jefferson's administration was the scene of confused excitement. There was grumbling against the embargo act, quarrels with England and France were in full sway and a presidential election was just around the corner. Talk of war was in the air while Congress prepared to enlarge the armed forces and fortify seaboard cities. An unusually large crowd of politicians was converging on the city, each seeking high rank in the new army. It was a setting most unsuitable for young Pike's talents, for, although he never hesitated to use political pressure, he

[2] New Orleans, Louisiana, September 17, 1807, Western Reserve Historical Society Archives.

was seldom successful. Moreover, his friendship for the now discredited Wilkinson must have been a serious handicap.

Legislation then pending in Congress, and destined for passage in the spring of 1808, would provide for an army of 32,800 troops, including militia. Soon after his arrival in Washington, on December 17, 1807, Captain Pike wrote to the Secretary of War: "I have conceived that I was at liberty to propose myself to the government as a candidate for the command of one of the corps to be raised."[3] He reminded the Secretary of his twelve years' service and his "vigor of mind" and, not forgetting a friend, proposed that Dr. Robinson be made a captain.

In neither project did he succeed. He did, however, eventually obtain an appointment to West Point for his younger brother, George Pike, now fifteen years of age. When the next term at the Military Academy opened in April, 1809, George was to be among the new class of forty-two plebes.

"Secure your independence by an early attention to economy without niggardness," Pike wrote to him, "—let your arms be the best—your clothes appropriate to your rank— and your behavior such as is becoming to the son of an old patriot and soldier—and the brother of a man not unknown to the army. Pay attention to your grammar and orthography —as the latter point you have made several mistakes in your letters to me: there is nothing which so certainly shews a want of education. You likewise use capitals too frequently. They are seldom properly used except at the beginning of sentences or proper nouns, if persons, places, or things. You see that I

[3] Z. M. Pike to General Henry Dearborn, Washington, D. C., December 17, 1807, War Records Division, National Archives.

[4] Z. M. Pike to George Pike, Washington, D. C., February 25, 1808, Western Reserve Historical Society Archives.

myself have committed many errors I caution you against—still I hope the advice will be received as coming from a brother."[4]

Although General Dearborn had refused Pike's request for a command in the new army, he did offer him the rank of major in the rifle corps—a position that could only mean a return to some western outpost—and Pike did not accept the offer with good grace. On April 14, 1808, he wrote to Dearborn vigorously protesting the proposed transfer, because it would place him under command of General Winchester, a man "heavy, dull, fat, unenterprising and incapable." Moreover, the lieutenant colonel of the corps would "doubtless be some rough backwoods Indian fighter with no ideas of organization or discipline." And Pike would be outranked by two men who "would reap all of the honor." "Could General Dearborn make me the Lieutenant Colonel of the Corps, I would serve with General Winchester *solely* from his having been a Revolutionary Officer."[5]

Pike's letter apparently went unanswered, for soon he was threatening to resign his army commission and accept the command of the New Jersey militia, a position lately offered him by the governor of the state. There he would not only become a general, but would be, as he phrased it, "the salve of the Regiment."[6]

However, Pike did not resign from the army. He was promoted to major in the Sixth Infantry, on May 3, 1808, and he commanded a small detachment at Bellefontaine from the

[5] Pike to Dearborn, Washington City, April 14, 1808, War Records Division, National Archives.

[6] "Salve" was a word commonly used at this time to mean "flattery" or "praise" (see *The English Dialect Dictionary*, edited by Joseph Wright, 1923); thus he would be the "pride" of the regiment. Pike merely was stating that he did not wish to share honors with any superior officer.

late summer until his transfer in December to Fort McHenry at Baltimore, Maryland.

While in Washington, Pike was also busily engaged in affairs other than political. He finished his full reports to the War Department and twice called at the White House, where he was "received with great attention and respect." Pike took this opportunity to obtain Jefferson's blessing on the publication of his journals. Jefferson believed such publication would be one means of acquainting the public with the newly purchased Louisiana region.

For the next few months Pike was busy editing his manuscript. In June, 1808, he procured copyright for a book entitled: *An Account of Expeditions to the Sources of the Mississippi, and through the Western Parts of Louisiana, to the Sources of the Arkansas, La Platte, and Pierce Juan, Rivers; performed by order of the Government of the United States during years 1805, 1806, and 1807. And a Tour through the Interior Parts of New Spain, when conducted through the Provinces by order of the Captain-General in the Year 1807.* Pike was nothing if not thorough.

In 1810, three years before publication of the Lewis and Clark journals, Pike's book was released from the press. Its publishers, C. and A. Conrad and Company of Philadelphia, employed John Binns, one of the foremost craftsmen of his day, to do the printing. Binns, according to tradition, had had the honor of being the first to print the Constitution. The original edition of Pike's journal contained a portrait of the author, a number of maps, reports, and charts, and a day-by-day account of his travels. According to the author's own statement in the foreword, "no book ever went to press under so many disadvantages."

Apparently the manuscript was printed in the same disorderly condition in which it had reached the publishers. Not only is it often dull reading, but it is marred by errors and contradictions which contrast sadly with the smoother style of the Lewis and Clark journals. The latter were not only better edited, but were prepared with more time and care.

Pike was handicapped by his lack of formal education. And in preparing his manuscript, he often had to rely on his memory, for many of his papers had been taken by the Spaniards. Nevertheless, one is amazed at the great quantity of the data the young explorer had brought back. His only aids were Dr. Robinson and the written reports of Lieutenant Wilkinson.

Soon after Pike's journal appeared, it was severely attacked by the famous geographer Alexander von Humboldt. "The maps of Mexico which are annexed to the narrative of his [Pike's] journey, are reduced from my great map of New Spain, of which I left a copy, in 1804, at the secretary of state's office at Washington."[7] This charge of plagiarism was neither admitted nor denied by Pike, but it must be remembered that standards of practice in such matters were not so generally recognized in his day as in ours.

Despite its many imperfections Pike's journal was well received by the public. In 1811 it was republished by a London firm, whose edition embodies some improvements over the original one. This edition was in turn translated into French, Dutch, and German, a tribute to the author and an evidence of the then very widespread interest in our great Southwest.

Not until Pike's book appeared was much national or international publicity given to his two expeditions. On July 16, 1811, the Washington *National Intelligencer* devoted three-

[7] Coues, *op. cit.,* xli–xlii.

fifths of a page to a summary of his Mississippi journey, derived from the published manuscript. Two days later the next issue gave four of its five columns to a discussion of the Arkansas trip. Doubtless these two accounts, and similar ones in other papers, added to Pike's fame and helped establish him as a world figure.

Typical of the reviews of Pike's book was the following: "We shall not attempt to criticise this useful volume with regards to its composition, or arrangement. He who wished to be acquainted with this interesting country, will not be offended at the plain style and minutiae of a diary. To the bulk of readers, the work would certainly have been more interesting if its diction were more polished, and its matter separated and arranged in a better manner. But our author has far exceeded our expectations, and he well merits the thanks of his countrymen."[8]

The years immediately preceding the War of 1812 were troubled ones for the young nation then struggling to make its democratic experiment a success. Strong leadership and superior statesmen were badly needed. Jefferson and Madison, though able, had limited experience and played the game of international politics with such amateurish abandon that we were finally swept, all unprepared, into a war with Great Britain.

Our military forces were composed of only two infantry regiments, one artillery regiment, and one corps of engineers until April, 1808, when Congress created eight new regiments in the regular army and enlarged the state militias.[9] As fast as the new troops were enlisted, they were dispersed to out-

[8] *National Intelligencer*, Washington, D. C., July 18, 1811, p. 1.
[9] *American State Papers*, VII, *Military Affairs*, I, 222–23.

posts along the Canadian border, on the Mississippi and the Ohio, and along the Atlantic and the Gulf. Most of these recruits were ill equipped, inexperienced, and untrained for fighting, and were fit only for policing the frontier, or for enforcing the embargo acts at our ports of entry.

Obviously these strategic harbors would be the first to feel the shock of enemy attack if war should be declared. New Orleans, which, because of its position at the mouth of the Mississippi, controlled the whole valley of that river, would be an irreparable loss should it fall to an enemy. So on December 2, 1808, Congress authorized the transfer to Lower Louisiana of the Third, Fifth, and Seventh Regiments of infantry, together with one battalion, or four companies, of the Sixth Regiment. Major Pike was put in command of the four companies and ordered to embark with them from Baltimore. Meanwhile, the Third, Fifth, and Seventh Regiments were to proceed overland.

Confident at last of fame and more promotions, Pike now put aside all threats of resigning. "My sword is always ready," he wrote a friend, "to defend the rights, and my life to be sacrificed to the great principles which have animated our forefathers—and which gave us a rank amongst the nations of the earth."[10]

It was Pike's business, as battalion commander, to obtain supplies, equipment, and transportation for his troops, a task which required his full attention over several weeks. On February 7, 1809, the Lexington *Gazette* carried a brief notice of the intended embarkation: "We understood that Major Pike has chartered several merchant vessels as transports to convey U. S. troops from this place [Baltimore] to New Or-

[10] Pike to Caesar A. Rodney, Baltimore, Maryland, December 12, 1808, Charles B. Pike Collection, Chicago Historical Society.

179

leans. It is said that several companies are expected from Carlisle, to embark in their transports. It is right to secure our vulnerable points, as well and as readily as possible; and this we perceive, from various orders and movements is about to be effected."

From Pike's personal letters it appears that he sailed sometime in January, 1809, for on December 20, 1808, he had written to his brother at West Point: "If you can obtain leave of absence, come immediately to Baltimore where you will see Clara and me. . . . If you do not arrive here by the middle of January, we shall be gone—where you cannot come."[11] Unfortunately, George was away on vacation at the time, and when the letter finally reached him, Pike and his family had already sailed.

They took passage on the *Minerva,* a small merchant vessel carrying 3,500 rations but few troops other than officers and their wives. Some ten or twelve vessels of similar size bore the remaining five hundred troops, their families, and the supplies. Pike's first extant letter about the trip, postmarked New Orleans, is dated June 4.

From this return to New Orleans in 1809 until his death in battle four years later, Pike's movements are easily traced. He was stationed at a number of posts in the South and the Northeast, performing a variety of duties. When the war with England began in 1812, few regular officers were more experienced or better trained for military leadership. He had been almost literally everywhere and had done everything in the little American Army.

New Orleans was a bustling, gay, and gaudy city of some 25,000 people—French, Spanish, Portuguese, Irish, Anglo-

[11] Z. M. Pike to George Pike, Baltimore, Maryland, December 20, 1808, Western Reserve Historical Society Archives.

Saxons, Negroes, Indians, and mulattoes. Thousands of flat-boats came down the river every year to deposit their cargoes of tobacco, whiskey, livestock, and produce, while sailboats, in daily procession, pushed upstream from the Gulf. Manufactured goods and human chattel were exchanged for the produce of western farms.

Here was a city of merchants, crooks, boatmen, intriguers, mulattoes, Choctaws, Creoles, aristocrats, slave traders, beggars, gamblers, dope addicts, soldiers, fine ladies, and tarts —in short, much of the "scum" and much of the "cream" of society. Often the dividing lines were blurred.

Situated some hundred miles above the river mouth, the "Creole City" was then almost wholly surrounded by a mud wall. Already it had a look of great age, its yellow stucco houses molding in the humid climate. Immediately to the south lay old Fort Charles, and forty miles on downstream, at the little village of Placquemines, was the dilapidated fortress of St. Philip, built by Spain in 1791.

East of Fort St. Philip, where Bayou St. John flows into Lake Pontchartrain, stood a more ancient redoubt erected by the French against the approach of any enemy by the lake. All of these were now in a state of decay, and Pike was assigned to help supervise their renovation.

For the better defense of New Orleans, President Jefferson had recommended to Congress as early as January, 1809, the digging of a canal from the Mississippi to Lake Ponchartrain "in order that vessels of both stations might unite and meet in conjunction an attack from either side," and another fortification to be erected near English Turn, some twelve miles below the city. General Wilkinson was now authorized to commence this work with all haste.

"His Serene Highness," as his "friends" in Louisiana

called Wilkinson, did not return to the scene of his former "triumphs" until April 19. Enroute from Baltimore, he had stopped at Havana to dispose of some private goods transported at government expense—and this in the face of the embargo. Both Wilkinson and Pike found a cool reception in New Orleans, despite the public clamor for troops and fortifications. Civilian and military co-operation, although badly needed, was not to be had, a condition common in the early days of the Republic.

By the late spring, troops in the New Orleans area numbered about three thousand, but more than half were sick and demoralized. The debilitating climate had brought fever and dysentery to some, while hundreds more were soon abed with venereal diseases. By May, only three doctors were well enough to treat the sick and dying, while the work of construction and repair had to be halted. Unless moved to a healthier region, this army would soon be unfit for further service.

Accordingly, William Eustis, now secretary of war, ordered Wilkinson to move his troops at once, suggesting, as a better site, Fort Adams, near Natchez. Disregarding this suggestion, Wilkinson chose instead to make a cantonment at Terre aux Boeufs, some twelve miles south of New Orleans. This site, he said, was dry, healthy, and not without strategic value. On May 29, Major Pike got his orders to set up the cantonment.

Only nine companies, four or five hundred men, were well enough to move. At Terre aux Boeufs, they faced the seemingly hopeless task of digging canals, constructing levies, and clearing a thirty-acre tract for the erection of tents and buildings. Undoubtedly the site was the worst possible for a permanent encampment. By day the men struggled through mud and filth, and by night mosquitoes denied them rest. Small wonder that in a short time the sick and dying outnumbered the able bodied.

Matters at Terre aux Boeufs grew worse before they improved. Mosquito nets were to be had, but only at $2.50, half a soldier's monthly pay. Flour molded in the humid climate, and the meat swarmed with maggots. Food could be had from New Orleans merchants only at exhorbitant prices. Wilkinson later complained that he was unable to buy "even the poorest cow for a hundred dollars."

Pike, much chagrined over conditions at Terre aux Boeuf, eventually procured a few barrels of flour and some meat, which, though of very poor quality, may have saved a few lives. Vegetables were not available at any price, chickens came at $7.50 a dozen, eggs at 37½ cents, and wine at $5.00, but such luxuries were only for the sick. Some medicine was obtained, but without doctors medicine alone proved of little value.

By some miraculous intervention Pike escaped illness at Terre aux Boeufs and was able to spend a good deal of time with his family in the city. Throughout the summer of 1809 he was busy obtaining supplies and sending them on to the cantonment. Not infrequently he was the only officer at Terre aux Boeufs to minister to the sick and bury the dead. The fact that he himself was not to blame for the loss of life there became apparent at a later Congressional investigation, in which several witnesses testified to his care for his men.

Yet, needless to say, the Louisiana newspapers could not let pass such an opportunity to further discredit both Wilkinson and Pike. On March 5, 1810, the *Natchez Chronicle* claimed that over 800 troops had died at Terre aux Boeufs in the previous summer, while from the *American State Papers*,

Military Affairs it is ascertained that the total number of troops who died in Louisiana from May 1, 1809 to February 28, 1810, was 686.[12]

"'Tis said," the *Weekly Chronicle* reported, "that the owner of the soil, has, or plans to make, to the proper person, suitable returns for the benefits his property has received." This charge was hard for Wilkinson to deny, for in the three months his troops were stationed at Terre aux Boeufs, the proprietor, one Jean Delassize, received $640.34, an unusually high rental when we remember that thirty acres of swampland had now been drained and could be planted with cane. Formerly "one of the foulest swamps on the banks of the Mississippi," its value was now increased many fold.

Self-righteously, Wilkinson played the role of persecuted martyr, testifying before a Congressional committee some weeks later that his every act had been guided by a tender care for his men. He had never had any business with Delassize or got any money from him for draining his land. Still the Louisiana press was not to be silenced. No immediate blame was attached to Pike, but his continued association with Wilkinson did his public reputation little good.

On June 22, 1809, Secretary Eustis ordered Wilkinson "to embark all of the troops, leaving a sufficient garrison of old troops at New Orleans and Fort St. Philip, and proceed with them for the high grounds in the rear of Fort Adams and Natchez." Wilkinson, delaying as usual, abandoned Terre aux Boeufs at long last that September.

Only three companies remained in New Orleans, and these were now put under command of Wilkinson's friend, Major Pike. "An old and respectable officer [Major McRae] has

---

[12] This mortality, whatever its true extent, can be attributed largely to General Wilkinson's callous venality.

the command of New Orleans Territory wrested from him," wailed the Natchez *Weekly Chronicle* (September 16, 1809), "to give it to a soldier of yesterday, a parasite of Wilkinson. . . . a junior officer is not appointed to the command of the capital for the purpose of promoting its 'security,' as is frivolously alleged in the order, but for having exerted every nerve to prop up the rotten fame of the Commander in Chief. . . . This is the first time we ever heard of the rank of a senior officer being unequal to that of a junior officer."

McRae, Pike's predecessor, had commanded the city's garrison for eighteen months, during which his frequent criticisms of Wilkinson had doubtless hastened his demotion.

Pike had reason to be pleased with his new command, for he could now remain in the city with his family. Clara Pike, great with her fifth child, would be unable to travel for several weeks.

The Major himself soon received additional responsibilities. "The situation of the public and the impossibility of finding a suitable character in private life to undertake the temporary duties of Military Agent, obliges me to impost that office on you," wrote General Wilkinson on September 13, 1809.[13] This position, usually held by a civilian appointed by the secretary of war, was like that of quartermaster general, the agent being authorized to purchase supplies, supervise construction of military works, and act as paymaster.

At first Pike pretended to be displeased with his new burdens, but he was soon trying hard to obtain the appointment on a permanent basis. Writing to the Secretary of War, he claimed to have uncovered much fraud in the records of his predecessors. He was sure that a military man would be more a suitable agent than any civilian. Secretary Eustis however,

[13] War Records Division, National Archives.

185

aware of Pike's unpopularity in New Orleans and fearful of political repercussions, refused to make the appointment permanent.

On December 31, Pike did nevertheless get a very welcome promotion. A lieutenant colonel was paid sixty dollars a month with substantial allowances. This, with his commissions as acting military agent, allowed Pike to live in a style more befitting his tastes. But his enemies would give him no peace, and he had other worries, too. Mrs. Pike was confined to her bed; his brother James, now in the city, was ill with tuberculosis; and his mother, at Lawrenceburg, Indiana, was thought to be close to death. Moreover, Pike's friends in the government were getting fewer. President Jefferson was no longer in office, General Dearborn had stepped out as secretary of war, and Wilkinson's continued friendship became more embarrassing every day.

Such was his situation when he received a distressing letter from his indolent younger brother, George. "Yours of the 6th ulto, dated West Point," Pike replied, "was duly received and astonished me beyond expression. You cannot study—and why, Pray? You may answer your unhappiness relative to your mother—and do you suppose you will add to her happiness by returning—to increase her embarrassment, to make her more so?

"Do you recollect with what ardour she exerted herself to get you off from home—with a fond hope. Yes, repeat 'with a fond hope' that you would exert yourself with much fortitude in a profession which had given a name to your family, which introduced you into the service with every possible advantage and favours. . . .

"And what does he prefer to this?—poverty—ignorance —and the contempt of the brave. And is this the youth for whose good conduct I have pledged myself—for whose honorable deportment the commander in chief of the American army has pledged his word? Is this my brother? No, it cannot be; some fatal delusion has spread itself over him—and he has not his reason. 'Oh! Almighty Father' restore him to his true sense,—let him see that fortitude is the first gift of the soul—without which we sink into the depths of bitterness and vice.

"You have written to the Secretary of War for five months pay—in advance! And have you lost your senses—do you not know that your letter will be treated with contempt; or sent to Col. Williams with orders to punish you for your impudence—madness, I should say.

"Oh! George—much I fear other causes than your anxiety to return home has been the cause of your present distress —Impudence. I did not expect you to remain clear of youthful follies—but—I fondly hoped you would not ruin yourself —sum up your courage if it is not too late—if your circumstances are embarrassed, say so to me—and to what amount— If I can help you I will."[14]

Pike may not have been aware of the true conditions at West Point, for in 1810, with morale and standards very low, the corps had dwindled to fifteen cadets and two instructors. Moreover, George was also ill with tuberculosis and had but a short time to live.[15]

At Christmas, 1809, Pike's mother died, a severe blow, coming as it did at the same time as the death of his own infant

[14] Z. M. Pike to George Pike, August 17, 1809, Western Reserve Historical Society Archives.

[15] George Pike graduated with seventeen classmates from West Point on March 1, 1811. Despite his brother's efforts to obtain an appointment for him in his own regiment, he was assigned instead to the Second Regiment. He died on February 21, 1812, at the age of nineteen.

child. Nor were his troubles ended: a short time later General Wilkinson, though exonerated by a Congressional committee, was removed for his bungling at Terre aux Boeufs and replaced by a sworn enemy, General Wade Hampton.[16]

No sooner had Hampton arrived than he removed Pike and exiled him to the Fourth Massachusetts Regiment in Mississippi Territory. "How are the Mighty Fallen," cried the Natchez *Weekly Chronicle* (March 5, 1810). "We learn with great pleasure that General Hampton has ordered Major Pike with all the infantry, to repair immediately to the cantonment near Washington, Mississippi Territory, and it is presumed that the veteran McRae, who was removed from the command of this city by general Wilkinson, to make room for the junior major, will resume his old command. It is also a curious fact, that the president has bestowed on Captain Swan, a genuine Wayneite [General Anthony Wayne, although now dead, was a former enemy of General Wilkinson's], the appointment of Military Agent, and thus disappointed the gold prospect of General Wilkinson's pet bully, the knight of Santa Fe.

"This act of general Hampton, and the appointment of Captain Swan, will doubtless give great satisfaction to the army, and blast the towering hopes of the pensioner's supporters and co-adjutors. This rebuff, however, will fill the junior major with philosophy to meet an investigation of his trip to Santa Fe, before the representatives of the nation."

[16] No sooner was Wilkinson acquitted by the committee than he was faced with other charges and tried by an army court-martial. Again, he managed to cheat justice, but by 1812 his reputation was ruined and his army career doomed. Only Pike continued to defend "the persecuted old veteran," stating that "I have never omitted any thing in my favor to serve him or ceased to assert his innocence and honor."

14

"A Soldier All My Life"

LIEUTENANT COLONEL PIKE remained at New Orleans, as acting military agent, until March, 1810. Letters to his friends and family show that he was busy with many routine affairs: supervising the civilian contractors who were renovating the old forts, paying the workers, obtaining food and medical supplies, and disposing of surplus property.

In the midst of all this activity, he took time to write once again to his brother George. "You may not yet have learnt the loss we have experienced by the loss of our dear mother who departed this sublimiary life on the 25th December last. In her loss we all have to deplore the loss of the most affectionate of mothers. But she was a Christian and died the death of the righteous. I pretend not to offer you consolation my dear Brother, for nothing but an assurance in our breasts that our dear mother is now enjoying a life of uninterrupted happiness—happiness without delay—could ever reconcile us to such an irrevocable misfortune."[1]

Doubtless the transfer to Natchez was a blow to Pike's pride, although he appears to have borne it with good grace.

[1] Z. M. Pike to George Pike, New Orleans, February 14, 1810, Western Reserve Historical Society Archives.

He was now attached to the Fourth Massachusetts Regiment, under Colonel John P. Boyd, a blustering soldier of fortune. Of him Pike wrote to his father that "his having made an independent fortune of 20,000 pounds per annum certainly can be no objections to him."[2] Yet no sooner was Pike here established than he began writing again to the Secretary of War, panting for advancement and declaring that he should long since have "resigned the sword and become a farmer."

If Pike had difficulty in obtaining promotions, at least his efforts were persistent. On June 10, 1810, he suggested to Secretary Eustis that if the Fourth Regiment should be consolidated and Colonel Boyd transferred, he would be "most happy to retain the command." Incidentally he pointed out that the recent battle of Jena had outmoded the strategy still employed by the United States Army—a fact which even the thick-headed Eustis should have perceived, but apparently did not. Pike promised that, were he given the command of the corps, he should at once introduce modern discipline, and make it "equal to any in the United States in one year." This would be no very difficult task, given the sordid state of military affairs in 1810.[3]

Several companies of the Fourth Regiment were then encamped at Washington in Mississippi Territory, six miles below the robust city of Natchez. During his months in this area, Pike wrote often to his aging father at Lawrenceburg, Indiana. Fortunately, some of these letters have been preserved and in them something of his thoughts in the months preceding war.

[2] Washington, Mississippi Territory, July 10, 1810, Western Reserve Historical Society Archives.

[3] Not until 1812 was Pike given the command of a regiment, and he then fulfilled his promise. His unit soon became "an example of zeal, discipline, and aptitude."

"Whether I shall remain here is uncertain," he wrote on July 10, 1810, "but I could not be more proudly situated in a military point of view than I am. If we have war it will be with France, which must be according to their own terms 'a la distance'—however, it will have the effect to unite us and cause us to rally round our government. . . . In all probability we shall have war, if so I shall remain a soldier all my life—for five or six years more would render me unfit for any other duty or profession, but I had recently become disposed to quit. Yet all my friends seem now to think I should remain, but the idea of always being poor is what I detest more, especially when I see so many worthless scoundrels men of fortune."[4]

In April, 1811, Pike was transferred to the command of troops at Baton Rouge, remaining there until recalled to the East in 1812 to take part in the invasion of Canada. While at Baton Rouge he was made a victim of army politics. Almost every officer who remained long in the service was at some time brought before a military court of inquiry, and Pike was to be no exception. Courts-martial were indeed so common that they seldom involved much reflection on the officer arrested and tried. The army had yet to learn that frequent courts-martial lessened efficiency by perpetuating little jealousies and hatreds. Each high officer had his particular followers, so that when one was arrested, several cliques might join the fray, some wishing to see him convicted and others vigorously defending him.

General Wade Hampton had replaced Wilkinson in command of the Southwest after the fiasco at Tierre aux Boeufs. During the spring of 1811, Wilkinson was brought before a

[4] Z. M. Pike to Zebulon Pike, July 10, 1810, Western Reserve Historical Society Archives.

military tribunal in Washington on charges of misconduct, negligence, treason, graft, and the waste of public funds. The "old veteran" counted heavily on the testimony of two character witnesses, Pike and Colonel Thomas H. Cushing. However, both were put under arrest by Hampton, causing Wilkinson to complain bitterly that his chief material witnesses were retained on "feigned pretenses" so that they could not testify in his behalf.

The only charge Hampton made against Pike was that of disrespect to his superior in announcing an as yet unauthorized list of promotions. On Pike's explaining his action, he was promptly released (May 2, 1811), but it was now too late for him to aid Wilkinson, just as Hampton had intended. The incident made Hampton and Pike enemies, and it was extremely gratifying to the latter to learn that, after all, the "persecuted old veteran would be honorably acquitted."

Colonel Cushing's arrest proved to be more interesting, because its story had an ironic climax. General Hampton accused him of opening mail, disobedience to orders, and general misconduct—charges that may have had some element of truth, inasmuch as Cushing remained several months under arrest. On November 2, 1811, Pike wrote to the attorney general, Caesar A. Rodney: "The general courts-martial should reassamble tomorrow to try another persecuted veteran, Cushing, but as we have not heard anything from his prosecutor Hampton, we are uncertain what will be the course."[5]

Cushing's case was not settled until March, 1812. He was found guilty and reprimanded, but his reputation did not suffer. Moreover, only a few weeks later, he was made adjutant general and in that capacity "repaid" his former friends

---

[5] Z. M. Pike to C. A. Rodney, Baton Rouge, November 2, 1811, Charles B. Pike Collection, Chicago Historical Society.

Sackets Harbour
April 23 1813

Sir

By this Days mail I had
the honor to receive the Appointment
of Brigadier General, which the President
of the United States has done me the
honor to confer on me. In conveying
my acceptance of the same I beg
leave through You Sir, to assure the
President that the tenure of my
future life, shall justify this flattering
proof of his confidence.—

I am Sir
with high Consideration
Your Obedt
Servt

Z M Pike

The Honorable John Armstrong
Secretary War Department

and enemies. Pike and his father (who had served with Cushing in the Revolution) got immediate promotions.

Some months after Pike's release, he met General Hampton face to face, when the latter arrived at Baton Rouge to inspect the military post. "He honored me by not offering his hand, and endeavoring to insult me by neglect and inattention," Pike wrote to his father.[6] But, as Hampton prepared to leave, he turned to Pike and remarked that his troops "manoeuvered in a style far superior to anything I could expect in our army," and that the general appearance of the post "meets with my highest approbation." Hampton's words were not only a tribute to his subordinate but a witness of his own magnanimity.

Happily most of Pike's time at Baton Rouge was absorbed in less personal matters. The daily record book of his post for 1811–12, now in the National Archives, contains a day-to-day account of routine affairs. The following passage taken from it is a typical example of the menial tasks he was forced to perform: "John Burnett of Captain Britter's company charged with repeadly following and abusing Polly Burnett, in camp and about Capt. Atchison's quarters, and particularly beating and abusing her on the morning of the 4th of October, 1811. Pled guilty of beating Polly Burnett on the 4th inst., but not guilty of the residue. The court find the prisoner guilty and sentence him to receive fifty lashes. The commanding officer approved of the foregoing and orders it to be carried into execution."

As the year 1811 drew to its close, the United States was drifting steadily toward war. After Tippecanoe, war hysteria

[6] Z. M. Pike to Zebulon Pike, Baton Rouge, December 20, 1811, Western Reserve Historical Society Archives.

surged across the Old Northwest, aroused by General Harrison's report that the Indians had had British guns and powder. The engagement was hailed as a great national victory and Harrison as a hero. Most of his regulars, however, had been trained by Pike in Mississippi. Their removal to the Northwest had occurred at the time of Pike's transfer to Baton Rouge, a transfer which deprived him of the glory of combat.

As war clouds thickened, Pike perceived that the army would be enlarged and rapid promotions be given its regular officers. Writing again to his friend Rodney, Pike dropped a subtle reminder that "should there be an augmentation of the army—shall I calculate on your influence my dear friend to promote my interest for promotion?"[7] As ill luck would have it, Rodney soon retired from the cabinet and apparently was unable to help his dear friend materially.

Meanwhile, Pike had a chance temporarily to sooth his lust for action with the sword, a weapon which had in fact gathered more rust in recent years than had his pen. The old Neutral Ground in the Southwest, between the Arroyo Hondo and the Sabine River, had again erupted into activity. Soon after Generals Wilkinson and Herrera had signed their agreement of 1806, establishing this neutral area, outlaws had begun moving in. Some had been former associates of Aaron Burr who took refuge here after their leader's arrest; some were the backwash of the United States and Mexico; and some were merely "squatters."

Within a short time the more disorderly element became so active that peaceful settlers often had to flee their homes. Late in 1807 the Spanish commandant at Nacogdoches (Texas) wrote to the American civil judge at Natchitoches (Louisi-

---

[7] Z. M. Pike to C. A. Rodney, Baton Rouge, November 2, 1811, Charles B. Pike Collection, Chicago Historical Society.

ana) suggesting a joint effort to drive out the brigands. This was actually done, but not until 1810. The Neutral Ground was not long to be safe for caravans plying between Natchitoches and Nacogdoches. By 1812 all commercial intercourse had ceased again, and American merchants were demanding action of Governor Claiborne.

This official at once wrote to General Hampton suggesting the erection of military posts between Natchitoches and Nacogdoches. Such an act, although it might protect American traders, would, as Hampton pointed out, be a violation of the Wilkinson-Herrera agreement. The General proposed, instead, another joint Hispano-American expedition like the one two years before. This being agreed upon, Hampton ordered Lieutenant Colonel Pike, on February 5, 1812, to proceed to Natchitoches with two companies of men.

Pike was further instructed to write the Spanish commandant at Nacogdoches, inviting his participation. He was to explain that if the invitation were refused, the Americans would proceed anyway but would in no case remain in the neutral area longer than needful. (The country could ill afford trouble with Spain when war with England was imminent.)

Pike arrived at Natchitoches before the end of February, and wrote at once to the Spaniard at Nacogdoches: "As my time here is limited and the matter is of the utmost urgency, I shall proceed with the troops of the United States alone to effect their objective if you do not approve the plan for cooperation."[8] The commandant, however, said he required the approval of the provincial governor before he could act; and

[8] Pike to Bernardino Montero, February 26, 1812, MS., Bexar Archives, University of Texas, Austin, Texas. For a full account of the Neutral Ground see Villasana Haggard, "The Neutral Ground Between Louisiana and Texas, 1806–1821," *The Louisiana Historical Quarterly*, Vol. XXVIII, No. 4 (October, 1945), and Harris G. Warren, *The Sword Was Their Passport.*

while word from San Antonio was pending, Pike sent two officers and forty mounted troops into the Neutral Ground. There they had no trouble in routing the outlaws, and within a few weeks the bandit camps were found and burned. Sixteen men, thirty-five horses, and quantities of "stolen" goods were captured.

"Pike," wrote John Sibley, the Indian agent at Natchitoches, "came here about two months ago & sent out Lieutenants Magee [later to lead the Gutiérrez-Magee filibuster into Spanish Texas when his followers would consist largely of the same neutral grounders whom he now routed] & Montgomery with about 40 men who patrolled the country as far as the Sabine laying everything to waste."[9]

Sibley compares the foray to "General Tauro's expedition to La Vendee and [the Americans] were endeavoring to imitate his recorded exploits among women & children."[10] Referring then to the projected invasion of Canada, he predicted that if the conduct and character of the troops be not changed, "the men, women, and children will arise in mass against them and be exterminated before they are conquered."

This invasion of the Neutral Ground by Pike added little to his popularity. Critics particularly denounced his treatment of the prisoners. Of those captured, two escaped, while fourteen were brought to Natchitoches for questioning and trial. Five were released as soon as their innocence was established. But one of them, Miguel Crow, complained that the

[9] Sibley to Major Amos Stoddard, April 2, 1812, Sibley Papers (typed copy), Missouri Historical Society Archives.

[10] Sibley refers to the French general, Louis Turreau, who in 1794 invaded La Vendee in western France. The peasants there had refused to support the French Revolution, and as a punishment, General Turreau systematically "scoured" the country, leaving it a "smoking desert." This brutal policy only goaded the inhabitants to a more desperate resistance.

troops had sacked his house, killed his livestock, and stolen his wife's earring. The fate of the nine retained was worse: "Some of them were stripd, tied to trees & whiped & burnt with chunks of fire (as they said) to make them confess."

Pike was back in New Orleans by March 1, preparing to sail for the East. On his request, Governor Claiborne supplied him with a letter of introduction to President Madison: "I beg the liberty to recommend to your future patronage, Lieutenant Colonel Zebulon Pike. He is in the vigor of life, about thirty-five years of age, and possessed of a healthy robust constitution. To an enterprizing spirit, he unites great perseverance, and the most cool and deliberate courage."[11]

Pike and his family must have arrived in Philadelphia early in May. He now wrote to Aunt Jeanet of the death of his mother and young brother George, and of his father's enfeebled condition. "James has returned home from New Orleans to die. Maria is married to a lawyer," he continued. He himself was about to enroll his nine-year-old daughter in a "very celebrated private school in Philadelphia."

"I am going then to the seat of the government, and if we have war, I shall march immediately to Canada and leave Mrs. Pike here. If not, I believe that we shall go home to see our friends." Observing that he had married the daughter of a rich Kentucky planter, Pike closed by regretting that he had got no property from the union and was himself "scarce enough for money."[12]

By June 4, 1812, he was in Washington, again soliciting promotion from the Secretary of War. Pike did not fail to

[11] W. C. C. Claiborne to President James Madison, Territory of Orleans, County of Attackapas, March 1, 1812, Letter Books of W. C. C. Claiborne, 65. Mississippi State Archives, Jackson, Mississippi.
[12] Pike to Mrs. Jeanet Pike Gage, Philadelphia, May 20, 1812, Pike Family Association.

remind Eustis that he was now one of the army's oldest lieutenant colonels in point of continuous service. "By the bill now
before the Senate for the reorganization of the army there will
be four additional Brigadier Generals wanting. I have understood that in the local arrangements, Tennessee, the Mississippi and New Orleans Territories will be entitled to one. As
the former state has received one general [Andrew Jackson]
and a colonel, I presume she will not claim this one also."[13]

Apparently he got no satisfactory answer, for on his return to Philadelphia he was still begging for advancement.
Over the next several weeks he was attached to the newly
created quartermaster general's department, busily engaged
in getting supplies, flags, arms, uniforms, and equipment for
the proposed invasion of Canada.

On July 4, 1812, he wrote from Philadelphia to the acting
adjutant general at Washington, one Alexander McCaleb,
again demanding promotion. Once more he cited his years of
military experience and complained that he had held the same
rank two years with no advance. Now, happily, the fortune
of politics had just elevated his old friend, Thomas H. Cushing, to the adjutant generalship, and on July 6 he, in turn,
made Pike a full colonel.

Twelve days later the new colonel was writing that he
could not decide between a new drab uniform trimmed in
green, or a gray one trimmed in black—the uniform of a
brigadier general. "Every private in the army carried a Mar-
shal's baton in his knapsack," Louis XVIII of France was to
remark. This was also true of Pike, but his optimism was premature, for almost a full year was to elapse before his next
promotion.

[13] Pike to William Eustis, Washington City, June 4, 1812, Charles B. Pike
Collection, Chicago Historical Society Archives.

Since the American Revolution, the country had been at peace with Europe and was now completely unprepared for war. In the words of Isaac Roach, a Pennsylvania volunteer under Pike in the York campaign of 1813: "After a peace of 30 years and entirely engrossed in trade, every means had been neglected to prepare for war. Fortifications in ruins—our Navy neglected—military science unknown, our army nominally about 6,000 men. The country divided in opinion. One half advocating British measures, the other French. No national feeling or true patriotism, until the declaration of war, which was carried on by that party called the Democrats and opposed by those called Federalists. Indeed with few exceptions the war was carried on to its termination by the Democrats and violently opposed by their own citizens who advocated the conduct of the British even during the struggle."[14]

At the outbreak of war the population of the United States was a little over seven million, so that raising a sizable force, such as Congress had authorized, should have been an easy task. Yet the army had only 6,744 regulars. There had indeed been recent efforts to make the armed services more attractive. A quartermaster department was created to administer supply. Flogging was abolished. The period of enlistment was reduced to nine months. And recruits were to have a sixteen-dollar bounty, with a cash bonus and 160 acres of land when honorably discharged. But the response was more than disappointing. According to James Ripley Jacobs, the newly appointed officers were with few exceptions grossly ignorant: "They stumbled along with their subordinates, simultaneously learning and teaching as best they knew." The discredited Wilkinson, despite his incompetence, was at this

14 "Isaac Roach's Diary, 1812–1847," MS, p. 9, Historical Society of Pennsylvania, Philadelphia.

moment the ranking general of the army. General Dearborn was old and sick, while General Alexander Smyth was little more than a bombastic braggart. All three were soon to cover themselves with shame. Those officers possessing real leadership had as yet had no opportunity to demonstrate their worth.

Despite Pike's unbounded ambition and unshakable faith in his own abilities, not bad attributes perhaps at that, he was clearly superior to most of his fellow officers. As one of his earliest biographers rightly observed, probably no officer in the army was "held in a higher estimation."[15]

[15] General Henry Whiting, a distinguished soldier and competent military critic, wrote a life of Pike which was published in 1845 as Volume V in Jared Sparks' *Library of American Biography*.

15

"My Fame or . . . My Death"

TWO WEEKS before Pike obtained his colonelcy, the United States had declared war on Great Britain because of her impressment of American sailors and her illegal blockade. It was now imperative that all corps be brought to full strength, and Congress further authorized the creation of ten new regiments. Colonel Pike was to have the new Fifteenth Regiment, yet to be recruited, which was to be attached to General Joseph Bloomfield's brigade.[1]

Despite their lack of preparation, the Americans were confident that they would win the war before the year was out. Military strategy called for an immediate invasion of Canada by three separate armies: the main thrust via Lake Champlain toward Montreal, and two supporting attacks from either end of Lake Ontario. Pike's regiment was to serve in the Montreal campaign under Dearborn.

On July 19, Colonel and Mrs. Pike left Philadelphia and arrived in Trenton, New Jersey, the next day. "I am making every exertion to collect together the recruits in this quarter and get the necessary clothing and camp equipment," Pike wrote to General Cushing.[2] As the new recruits came in, they

[1] Bloomfield was soon destined for "innocuous obscurity."

[2] Z. M. Pike to Cushing, July 20, 1812, War Records Division, National Archives.

were sent to Staten Island, where the commander expected to join them soon.

"I leave here this day to join my Regiment (15)," Pike wrote to Wilkinson. He assured the General that his old friends were not neglected—most had received important assignments and promotions. It was well poor Pike could not foresee the sorry showing these worthies would make.

"Mrs. Pike is going campaigning with me," he continued, "but I have fixed her a place here to retire to and I find my New Jersey friends kind and polite—in fact I only want a little more money to make me a happy dog. If we go into Canada, you will hear of my fame or of my death—for I am determined to seek the 'Bubble' even in the cannon's mouth. Clara joins me in love to Mrs. Wilkinson."[3]

If Pike dreamed of a hero's death, it was because he believed that only through it could he achieve the everlasting fame his heart desired. He was soon to have that rendezvous with destiny, but he could have no prescience that, with this wish granted, he would be remembered not as a military figure but as the discoverer of a western peak.

When the Colonel reached New York late in July, he found there a letter from General Cushing: "You will please to take the immediate superintendence of the recruiting service for your own regiment. Order all the officers belonging to it to assist you in your duty. Appoint a suitable and convenient place for assembling and disciplining the men. Report your strength and progress weekly to Major General Dearborn at Albany and obey his orders. . . . Permit me to add that the

[3] Z. M. Pike to Wilkinson, July 24, 1812, Charles B. Pike Collection, Chicago Historical Society Archives.

interest of the country and the honor of the army, imperiously calls for the utmost exertions of recruiting officers."[4]

With the letter came a set of regulations governing the physique of new recruits. They were to be "free from sore legs, scurvy, scalded heads, ruptures, and other infirmities." Size would not matter if the man were strong and active. Boys from fourteen to eighteen would be accepted only with their parents' consent, and then only as musicians—drummers and fifers. Each recruiting officer was to be responsible for the conduct of his own recruits. He must further obtain the necessary supplies, food, and transportation for them, but he would be paid a bounty on their total number.

By August 2, the strength of the Fifteenth Regiment had been increased to six or seven hundred men. But converting a mob into an army has never been an easy task. It was a particularly trying one in 1812, when very little equipment, food, medical supplies, and clothing could be had. There was corruption, too. Pike himself lost no time in complaining to his superior, General Bloomfield, about the sordid conditions on Staten Island. Bloomfield, however, was incompetent or indifferent, for he offered no effective aid.

After training his men less than one week, Pike received orders from General Dearborn to transport them to Albany. Here the army was to be assembled for further training.

Sailing, however, was delayed for another week while the Colonel sought flints for his rifles; and the men, meanwhile, had no opportunity for target practice. Some, indeed, had never fired a gun in their lives. On August 11, Pike assured General Armstrong at Albany that his regiment would depart in a day or two and requested for himself the use of a small

---

[4] Cushing to Z. M. Pike, Washington City, July 31, 1812, War Records Division, National Archives.

sloop, left behind by General Bloomfield. It was no larger than a good barge but had a "nice cabbin on deck." "I would be pleased with the indulgence of taking her to Albany for the accommodation of myself and lady and will send her back if required."[5] So Clara Pike accompanied her husband to Albany and later on to Plattsburg.

By the end of August, Dearborn's army in upper New York numbered some thousand troops, with new recruits arriving daily. But when Pike reached Camp Greenbush, across from Albany, he found much yet to be desired. Some troops were without shelter or supplies, and the drill field was a freshly cleared area still encumbered with stumps and brush piles. Issac Roach arrived with a company of Pennsylvania volunteers a few days later to find the Inspecting General himself, Alexander Smyth, drilling a body of troops. Smyth, soon to resign in disgrace, was "standing cross-legged reading the words of command from a book, which was all we had to aid us in our discipline."

The initial invasion of Canada began on July 12, 1812, when General William Hull crossed the river from Detroit, only to fall back a few days later. On August 16, he surrendered Detroit without firing a shot. News of this fiasco shattered American hopes of an early victory and further depressed the drooping morale of the army. "I will not say one word about Hull's capture," Pike wrote to General Cushing, "as every American's feelings on that subject must be the same."[6]

On October 13, a yet worse disaster overtook the attack-

[5] Pike to Brigadier General John Armstrong, Staten Island, New York, August 11, 1812, War Records Division, National Archives.

[6] Pike to Cushing, September 2, 1812, War Records Division, National Archives.

ing forces at Niagara. Meanwhile, Colonel Pike and his regiment had marched overland to Plattsburg. Preparations were now really under way for the main offensive, against Montreal, sixty-three miles to the north.

General Dearborn expected to enter Canada with two brigades, the First under General Joseph Bloomfield, and the Second under General John Chandler. Colonel Pike's Fifteenth Regiment, together with the Sixth and the Sixteenth, made up the First Brigade. By the opening of September more than six thousand regulars and militia had been assembled at the cantonment on the Saranac River, not far from Plattsburg. Supplies, equipment, and food were furnished by private contractors, whose chief concern was profit.

Pike wrote repeatedly to his superiors and to the Secretary of War, lamenting the bad quality of goods supplied by these purveyors, particularly by one Tench Coxe. These protests unanswered, he took one of the blankets issued, folded it into a large envelope and sent it to General Eustis at Washington. The blanket, four feet by three, was an example of the only covering each man would have on a winter campaign in the North.

On November 16 the army encamped near Plattsburg began its march toward Canada. Traveling light, the troops reached Champlain, twenty miles north of Plattsburg and near the southern boundary of Quebec Province, before the end of the first day. There they halted, erected huts from fresh-cut spruce, and cleared a parade ground. On the following day Colonel Pike and six hundred men advanced eight miles into Quebec, and at ten o'clock, on November 21, encountered a small force of Canadian and Indian troops.

After a few shots, the enemy fell back to a swamp, and Pike proceeded to burn their barracks and blockhouses. As

205

the Americans were returning to Champlain, they came on another body of their countrymen, and each group, supposing the other to be an enemy, promptly opened fire. Six men were wounded, two of whom later died. These actions were Pike's first actual experience under fire. (It is doubtful whether he was ever in the presence of the enemy during Anthony Wayne's campaign in 1794–95.)

On the day following this reconnaissance, General Dearborn ordered his troops at Champlain to prepare for a three days' march. Supposing they were now to go to Montreal, they hastily cooked and packed and were all ready to move by eight in the morning.

When at last the order came, two hours later, what was their dismay to learn that they were going—not on to Montreal—but back to Plattsburg! Why Dearborn ordered such a retreat, nobody knows. Most historians state that his men refused to fight on foreign soil, since they had volunteered only to defend the United States. But Cromwell Pearce, commander of the Sixteenth Regiment, records in his memoirs that Dearborn's order "occasioned much mourning."[7] In any case the troops were back at Plattsburg on November 23, and the main invasion of Upper Canada now had to be postponed until spring.

Five days later they began the construction of log barracks for winter quarters a few miles above the previous encampment, on the Saranac. Until their completion on Christmas Day, the men were obliged to sleep on frozen ground, exposed to snow and sleet and protected only by their thin blankets and the fresh-cut branches of pine trees.

Long before permanent shelters were completed, most of the officers had rejoined their families. Colonel Pearce of the

[7] "Biographical Memoirs," 1855, MS, Historical Society of Pennsylvania.

Sixteenth and Colonel Pike of the Fifteenth remained the only high officers at hand to give orders and supervise construction. Morale and discipline vanished. There were riotous drinking, brawls, and sometimes murder. Many men died of exposure and neglect, among them about one hundred from Pike's regiment in the month of December alone.

Most of the blame should be attached to General Dearborn, long since corrupted by politics and unmanned by easy living. That any of his army still existed in the spring was due largely to the exertions of Pike and Pearce. Their task was a hard and thankless one. Desertions were frequent and threats of mutiny constant. All the help Pike got from Washington was this order from the Inspecting General: "If an officer shall mutiny, and it cannot otherwise be suppressed, the superior officer may kill or maim him while he resists. If a soldier shall mutiny, any officer or non-commissioned officer present shall seize the first musket he can lay hold of and break it over the offender's head."[8]

Late in December, Pike, too, became sick and had to spend several days in bed at Plattsburg while Mrs. Pike looked after him. On New Year's Day he wrote to Adjutant General Cushing explaining his absence from the regiment and complaining that the mortality among troops on the Saranac had already surpassed the deaths at Terre aux Boeufs in 1809.

He returned to his regiment resolved to reorganize it along the lines of a French unit. The Fifteenth soon "became an example of zeal, discipline, and aptitude in movement." Its officers and men acquired a respect for their commander's ability and a confidence in his leadership notably absent in the other regiments.

[8] A copy of this order was found in General Pike's official correspondence in the War Records Division, National Archives.

Since the Revolution, the United States Army had followed Steuben's now obsolete *Manual of Arms*. Casting it aside, Pike adopted the French practice of forming his men into three ranks, the third being armed with short guns and long pikes, which served as bayonets. His fellow officers might joke about "Pike's regiment of pikes," but the troops made nevertheless a quite impressive appearance, maneuvering with the "precision of automata."

Unfortunately the pikes were less effective on the battlefield. After their first experience in action, the men abandoned this weapon so as to deploy more effectively.

As the spring of 1813 approached, plans for the invasion of Canada were renewed. Congress created six new major generals and as many brigadier generals, and authorized six new regiments. Public opinion forced the removal of Secretary Eustis. And once again Pike fervently sought promotion.

To his aged friend Caesar Rodney, now living in retirement at Wilmington, he wrote: "I have understood from Washington that I am held up there as a candidate to fill a Brigade appointment. Will you lend a word (if you write) to some of your old friends at Washington to help me along?"

Secretary Eustis, Pike continued, "was a gentleman whom I highly respected—he was my friend and I strove to return the obligations. Yet I do not think he was calculated to be at the head of the War Department at the present day. As a man he was personally firm, as a public officer trembling at every act. General Armstrong, who now governs the destines of the War is in my estimation one of the two men (who come within my knowledge of able Americans) the most proper for the appointment. The other is Wilkinson."[9]

This estimate of Armstrong proved too optimistic, for he

Sackett's Harbor, *c.* 1813
Pike cantonment at the extreme left, Fort Tompkins to its right

Death of GENERAL PIKE
from a contemporary print in the New York Public Library

soon showed himself to be little, if at all, more effective than his predecessor. As for Wilkinson, Pike must have been almost the only man in the Republic who retained faith in his character and abilities. Pike was oddly defective as a judge of men, and Wilkinson was ever his blind spot.

General John Armstrong, if he lacked capacity, was at least a man of energy. In February he ordered General Dearborn to assemble four thousand troops at Sacketts Harbor, New York, and three thousand at Buffalo, for a two-pronged offensive against Canada. Its immediate objectives were to be the well-garrisoned shipbuilding centers of Kingston and York, at opposite ends of Lake Ontario.

Sacketts Harbor, strategically situated opposite Kingston and about eighteen miles from the mouth of the lake, was a fast-growing little town of some three thousand people. Here were constructed most of the ships of the Lake Ontario fleet. Guarding its harbor was a well-fortified battery, Fort Tompkins, consisting of four blockhouses surrounded by a thirty-foot limestone wall.

Colonel Pike left Camp Saranac on March 4 with all the men of his regiment then able to travel. Snow and ice still covered the ground, and, recalling his experience on the upper Mississippi, he had equipped his men with snowshoes and got them some large sleds for the transport of equipment. Unhappily, the former experiment, like that of the pikes, had to be abandoned, for the snowshoes here proved more a handicap than an aid.

Clara Pike remained at Plattsburg, expecting to join her husband on the northern front as soon as conditions might permit.

---

[9] Z. M. Pike to C. A. Rodney, Cantonment Saranac, January 24, 1813, Charles B. Pike Collection, Chicago Historical Society Archives.

On March 7, Pike, then with his troops at Chateaugay, New York, instructed Colonel Pearce to select 246 men from the Sixth and Sixteenth Regiments and follow the same route, via Malone. "God send you do not meet with the difficulties I have. One man was froze to death, last evening; and many wretches will loose their feet. I call them wretches—for intoxication is the principal cause."[10] Before the long march to Sacketts Harbor was accomplished, many more had died of exposure, for the snow lay often three or four feet deep.

Ten days after leaving Plattsburg the Fifteenth arrived and encamped a mile east of Fort Tompkins. Before permanent log barracks could be constructed, the fort being too small for more than a few hundred, windbreaks were made for temporary shelter. These structures were open on the south, and at night the soldiers built big fires in front of them. By March 25, they could move into the newly completed barracks.

Meanwhile, Pike had received word of his appointment as inspector general of the northern army and commander of Fort Tompkins. He set up his headquarters in one of the blockhouses and with characteristic energy prepared for the coming campaign. On April 5, official notice arrived of his promotion to brigadier general.[11]

For some reason a story has gained currency that Pike refused the new rank unless his father be likewise advanced. There is no authority to support the tale, and it is hardly in keeping with Pike's known persistence in demanding earlier promotions. Moreover, he seems to have been reconciled to his father's failing memory and consequent unfitness for any responsible post.

[10] Pearce, "Biographical Memoirs," 1855, MS, *loc. cit.*

[11] Pike was first brevetted a brigadier general (by Dearborn) in March on his arrival at Sacketts Harbor. The Senate did not confirm his permament promotion until about a month later; and meanwhile he had been killed in action.

Although Pike had worked hard to earn his new rank, it is doubtful whether he would have got it had it not been for the indolence of General Dearborn. This officer, instructed to lead the advance into Canada, had pretended illness and had ordered Pike to conduct the attack against York, in the capacity of a brigadier general. Later Dearborn was to claim for himself much of the credit of this successful operation.

More than 4,000 troops, including several companies of marines, had been assembled at Sacketts Harbor by the end of March. They were to cross Lake Ontario and assault York as soon as the ice broke, with Pike's First Brigade leading the attack. This rather miscellaneous unit of 1,700 men embraced the Sixth, Fifteenth, and Sixteenth Regiments, a company of light artillery, one company of the Fourteenth and another of the Twenty-first Regiments, Forsyth's Rifle Corps, one company of volunteers from New York and another from Baltimore.

York, present-day Toronto, had now been chosen instead of Kingston as the first objective, because it was thought to be less heavily fortified. It was the seat of government of Upper Canada and was about the size of Sacketts Harbor. Isaac Chauncey, who had insisted upon the initial blow at York, was to get the men across in a naval quadron under his command.

By April 20, the ice had melted enough to let the unit sail. The troops were to embark in thirteen vessels, one of them the newly completed *Madison*, a sister ship to the *General Pike*, still under construction at Sacketts Harbor and not yet named in the General's honor.

Before embarking, Pike had personally worked out the plan of attack. His orders were given to each field officer, who in turn was to read them carefully to his own corps. Personal property was to be respected and plundering forbidden. "The

General confidently hopes that the blood of an unresisting or yielding enemy will never stain the weapons of the soldiers of his column."[12]

To his father, Pike wrote: "I embark tomorrow in the fleet at Sacketts Harbor at the head of fifteen hundred choice troops, on a secret expedition. If success attends my steps, honor and glory await my name—if defeat, still shall it be said we died like brave men; and conferred honor even in death on the American name."[13]

The squadron sailed on April 23, and three days later anchored offshore opposite York. An unexpected storm had delayed the attack one day, and because of adverse winds, the fleet was unable to approach nearer than a mile and a half below the town and half a mile offshore. At seven o'clock on the morning of April 27, the first landing craft, embarking parts of the Fifteenth and Sixteenth Infantry and all of Forsyth's rifles, started for shore.

The landing was not unlike a modern amphibious operation: naval vessels first laid down a barrage, to be followed by a wave of small boats, which discharged their men and returned to the ships for more. Some of the smaller craft, hit by shore batteries, capsized in the water, but most accomplished their mission safely. Enemy riflemen at the water's edge fired on our troops as they disembarked, but as more Americans came on, they stormed the beach with fixed bayonets, driving the defenders back to the woods, into which they now pursued them.

General Pike, among the first to land, urged his men on, while among the defenders the many Indian contingents were

[12] War Records Division, National Archives.

[13] Z. M. Pike to Zebulon Pike, April 22, 1812, Charles B. Pike Collection, Chicago Historical Society Archives.

now utterly demoralized. "Too much Yankee! Too much Yankee," they cried, throwing down their arms and fleeing in all directions.

Pushing on toward the town, the United States troops overran enemy batteries one after another, taking some almost without resistance. Meantime the ships offshore had concentrated their fire upon the fort guarding the town, while Pike and his men advanced to within four hundred yards of its wall. There he halted on the edge of a clearing so that his troops might bring up artillery.

General R. H. Sheaffe, the British commander at York, aware that further resistance was useless, now raised a white flag. As firing from the water ceased, Pike ordered one of his men forward to learn whether the enemy would agree to a formal surrender. Meanwhile, he himself helped an injured man to the rear and, returning to the edge of the clearing, sat down to await the British commander's reply. Now that the excitement was over, he felt exhausted. While his staff gathered round him to discuss the recent action, a soldier, coming up from the rear, declared that he had a British prisoner for questioning.

Before the General could reply, a terrific explosion rent the air. A near-by British magazine, abandoned by the enemy, had blown up, scattering rocks, timber, and debris for hundreds of yards. As the dust cleared, Colonel Pearce, who had been some fifteen paces away, found General Pike lying prone and heard him exclaim that his injury was mortal. Indeed, a rock had torn a great hole in his back, and it was now plain to all that the gallant soldier could not live.

Before he was carried away, Pike gave the command to Pearce and, turning his head toward the soldiers gathering round him, weakly cried, "Push on my brave fellows and avenge your general." The wounded man was then carried back to the *Madison* and laid upon a cot, a captured British flag beneath his head. From shore there came to him already the shouts of victory, and he smiled at the thought that York was now his, the British had been routed.

He died on the lake a few hours later, en route to Sacketts Harbor. Legend has it that his body, for the sake of preservation, was placed in a hogshead of whiskey. At Sacketts Harbor it was taken ashore "with stately pomp," placed in an iron casket, and appropriately buried, while "flags were flown at half-mast, guns fired, music played, and a large procession marched."

For some years, Pike's grave in the cemetery outside Fort Tompkins was marked only by a crude wooden slab. In 1819, on completion of Madison Barracks, his body, along with others in the burying ground, was moved to the new post cemetery. A larger wooden marker was now set up to identify the graves of Pike and his military aide, Captain Joseph Nicholson, who was killed in the same explosion.[14] Unfortunately, the markers were neglected, and within a few years the exact place of Pike's burial was forgotten.

In 1909 the whole graveyard had to be moved again because of frequent floods. This time the bones were reinterred about half a mile east of Sackets Harbor.[15] Of 130 bodies, only four were identified, and Pike's was not among them. However, his was probably the one found in an iron casket, topped with glass and apparently filled with alcohol. When this casket was moved, the glass was broken, and the body within, now exposed to air, at once disintegrated.

[14] Pearce says 38 men were killed by the explosion and 222 wounded.
[15] Since 1900 Sacketts Harbor has been spelled "Sackets" Harbor.

Some years later the grave believed to be Pike's was identified with a small granite marker on a base of limestock rocks, and a bronze mortar, bearing a simple inscription, at present rests atop the marker. At this writing the Colorado Springs Chamber of Commerce is seeking the removal of Pike's body to the peak that bears his name, where a splendid monument is to be erected.

Although Madison Barracks is now surplus property and the government has consented to the removal of bodies interred there, it is unlikely that the people of Sackets Harbor will part with these famous bones. "General Pike's been buried here for more than a century," says the mayor, "and we mean to keep him here."[16]

The Battle of York was one of the United States' first victories in the War of 1812 and may be rightly considered the third most important engagement of the conflict.[17] Jackson's victory at New Orleans was more spectacular, but it occurred after the signing of a peace and had no effect upon the outcome of the war. Harrison's victory at the Thames, on October 5, 1813, however, clearly outranks in importance the taking of York. Both Jackson and Harrison were hailed as heroes and later attained the nation's highest civil office. Pike, had he lived, might also have become prominent in national politics, for he was not lacking in ambition.

When news of his victory was reported in the paper's Pike's name was imprinted on the mind of every American. The press was filled with eulogies, President Madison paid him special tribute in an address to Congress, and a newly

[16] *Time*, Vol. LI, No. 19 (May 10, 1948), 25.

[17] The British losses at York were estimated at 1,300 killed, wounded, and captured.

completed warship at Sacketts Harbor was christened *General Pike*.[18]

On June 5, *Niles' Register* paid him a glowing tribute following a detailed account of the battle: "His memory shall live, and be with us many generations."

And in the same issue appeared an account of a recent demonstration at the Baltimore Theater: "Between the second and third acts of the play the curtain slowly, but unexpectedly, rose to the solemn music, and exhibited a lofty oblisk on which was inscribed 'Z. M. Pike, Brigadier General—Fell Gloriously before York—March [April] 27, 1813.' . . . To the left of the monument was that elegant actress, Mrs. Green, dressed as Columbia, pointing with her spear, as she knelt on one knee, to Pike's name. On the other side was a lady dressed in an uncommonly splendid attire, with an expression on her face that expressed all the solemn magesty of woe. . . . As the curtain fell slowly to the floor, the people burst forth in one magnimous expression of applause."

On April 24, 1814, a board of honor of the Fifteenth Regiment met at Burlington, New Jersey, and passed the following resolution: "May the omnipotent hand which directs all things, cause his spirit to hover around our councils in the field, and at all times be with his beloved regiment." They further decreed that on each succeeding April 27, the Regiment's standard should be dressed in mourning, each officer wear crepe, and no duties be performed.

Since Pike's death, his name has not been forgotten. James Flint, a French traveler in the West in 1818, found his portrait commonly displayed in frontier taverns.[19] Ten counties,

---

[18] She was completed in time to take part in the last naval engagement on Lake Ontario when, meeting the *Wolfe* on September 28, 1812, she defeated her in a battle called the "Burlington Races."

in as many states, and eighteen towns and villages now bear his name, as do also two bays, three rivers, and at least four lakes. A number of states have erected monuments or placques to his memory, and Colorado is planning a new state park to be named for her first American explorer.

A few weeks after the taking of York, an account of Pike's death appeared in *Niles' Register*. His last words were: "I am mortally wounded—my ribs and back are stove in—write my friend D . . . and tell him you know of the battle—and to comfort my . . . ." To his wife, on the night before, he had written: "My dear Clara, we are now standing on and off the harbor of York, which we shall attack at daylight in the morning: I shall dedicate these last moments to you, my love, and tomorrow throw all other ideas but my country to the wind. As yet, I know not if General Dearborn lands; he has acted honorably so far, and I feel great gratitude to the old gentleman: My sword and pen shall both be exerted to do him honor. I have no new injunctions, no new charges to give you, nor no new ideas to communicate; yet we love to communicate with those we love, more especially when we conceive it may be the last time in this world. Should I fail, defend my memory, and only believe, had I lived, I would have aspired to deeds worthy of your husband. Remember me with a father's love, a father's care, to our daughter; and believe me, with the warmest sentiments of love and friendship,

Yours,
Montgomery."

[19] James Flint, *Letters From America*, in Thwaites, *Early Western Travels*, IX, 161.

Bibliography

I. MANUSCRIPTS

The most important manuscript materials throwing light upon
Zebulon Montgomery Pike's early career and family background
are the records of the Pike Family Association, West Newton,
Massachusetts. For the most part these records consist of an odd
assortment of genealogy charts; personal letters from Pike's descendants to the secretary of the Association, Mrs. Roscoe M.
Packard; copies of early newspaper stories about General Pike;
and miscellaneous information and family lore. In addition, there
is one important lengthy letter written by General Pike on May
20, 1812, to his Aunt Jeanet Pike Gage, in which he divulges
considerable information about his career, his parents, his wife,
and his children.

Approximately seventy-five or eighty items, consisting of letters, affidavits, and financial statements are found in the Division
of Pension Records, National Archives, Washington, D. C., which
contain considerable information about General Pike's father,
Major Zebulon Pike. These documents are dated from 1823 to
1828, and for the most part are written by Major Pike or close
friends in an effort to secure a pension for the elder Pike. Rather
complete details of Major Pike's career and experiences are given
in the various documents, which also furnish interesting side lights
and details about the entire Pike family.

The Charles B. Pike Collection in the Chicago Historical Society Archives contains an assortment of approximately two dozen
letters and papers written between July 21, 1780, and March 31,

1812. At least half of these documents are letters from Pike to his father, to General James Wilkinson, to William Eustis, the secretary of war, to C. A. Rodney, adjutant general, and to George Pike, the General's younger brother. From the collection I obtained many personal facts about Pike's life and military career.

In the Western Reserve Historical Society Archives, Cleveland, Ohio, is a small collection of Pike correspondence. It is filed under the category "Correspondence of General Pike," and its various letters range in date from October 12, 1801, to July 24, 1812. The letters are to Pike's father, mother, sister, and brothers, and more than any other source they give an intimate picture of Pike's personal ambitions, character, triumphs, and disappointments.

The most voluminous collection of Pike materials is in the National Archives, Washington, D. C. The War Records Division alone contains more than two hundred items, dating from 1805 to 1813, most of which consist of correspondence among General Pike, General Wilkinson, and various government officials. For the most part these documents relate to Pike's two western expeditions, but a number concern his subsequent military career, when he was stationed at various posts in Louisiana, Mississippi Territory, New Jersey, Pennsylvania, and New York. Nineteen of the twenty-one documents confiscated from Pike by the Spaniards in 1807 are included in the collection. These personal papers reveal little information that is not found elsewhere; they are more valuable for their history than their contents. Also included in the collection is the General Order Book, Headquarters, Baton Rouge. The entries in this book, most of which are signed by Pike, range in date from March 31 to December 17, 1811.

Correspondence relating to the search, discovery, and return of General Pike's personal papers which were confiscated by the Spaniards is scattered throughout various divisions of the National Archives. Several hundred letters, dating from 1906 to 1910, written by various members of Congress, and officials of the State Department and the American embassies in Spain and Mexico, were examined. The larger part of this correspondence is found in the division of Records of the Department of State, filed under the category "Numerical File, XXXIII, 1906–1910." Also, the Records of the Office of Adjutant General, War Records Office ("Document File"), and the Records of the Foreign Service Posts of the Department of State, American Embassy, Madrid, Spain ("Miscellaneous Letters"), contain many papers relating to Pike's lost documents.

The Bexar Archives, University of Texas, Austin, Texas, has approximately twelve letters, dating from February 26 to March 23, 1812, written in English and Spanish, which deal with Pike's journey into the Neutral Ground in 1812. This correspondence was conducted between Zebulon Montgomery Pike on behalf of the United States Army and Captain Bernardino Montero of the Spanish Army.

Additional manuscript material relating to Pike's experiences in the Neutral Ground was found in the John Sibley Papers in the Missouri Historical Society Archives, St. Louis. John Sibley, in letters written between June 30, 1807, and April 2, 1812, makes several references to Pike's two western expeditions, his capture by the Spaniards, and his conduct in the Neutral Ground in 1812. Much of Sibley's comment is critical of the explorer. Additional Pike material was found in the Amos Stoddard Collection of the Missouri Historical Society Archives, and several other miscellaneous items were uncovered in the same archives in which Pike's name is mentioned.

"The Biographical Memoirs of Colonel Cromwell Pearce," is a forty-eight-page unpublished manuscript in the library of the Historical Society of Pennsylvania, Philadelphia, which contains an excellent and informative account of General Pike's experiences in New York and Upper Canada from 1812 to 1813. The writer, one of Pike's fellow officers, gives a realistic picture of the sordid conditions in the army at the time, an evaluation of Pike as a commander, and a detailed account of the Battle of York in which General Pike was killed.

An unpublished diary kept by Isaac Roach (1812–47) is also found in the library of the Historical Society of Pennsylvania, Philadelphia, which contains several references to General Pike and the War of 1812.

In the Division of Manuscripts, Library of Congress, there are a number of Spanish documents relating to Pike's expedition to the West in 1806–1807, and his subsequent capture by the Spaniards. For the most part these documents consist of correspondence between Spanish officials in Mexico and in Spain. They are in Spanish script and are difficult to decipher, but from them one obtains a clear view of the Spanish suspicion of Pike's activities in the West. The materials consist of 311 pages and are filed under the following categories: "Archivo Histórico Nacional, Madrid. Estado. Legajo 5547–5548"; and "Secretaría de Guerra y de Marina, Mexico. Seccion de Various Asuntos. Legajo 1787–1807."

The William C. C. Claiborne Papers, in the Mississippi Department of Archives and History, Jackson, include eight letters either to Zebulon Montgomery Pike or in which he is mentioned. They range in date from February 8, 1811, to October 21, 1814, and reveal the close relationship between Pike and Governor Claiborne.

The Louisiana State Archives at Baton Rouge also contain a few documents in which General Pike's name is mentioned. This material adds little knowledge to Pike's activities in Louisiana, however. The collection includes seven Pike items, which are catalogued under the title: "Greenburg Land Claims, British West Florida, U. S. Land Office."

2. FEDERAL DOCUMENTS

Federal documents examined by the author bearing upon Pike's military career, the United States Army, and the War of 1812 are principally the *American State Papers: Military Affairs*, I; *Foreign Relations*, I; *Indian Affairs*, I; and *Miscellaneous*, I. Also, several references are made to Pike's western expeditions in the *Annals of Congress*, 7 Cong., 1 sess.; 11 Cong., 2 sess., Part I; 12 Cong., 1 sess., Part II.

In addition, the *Debates and Proceedings of Congress*, 10 Cong., 2 sess., Appendix, contains a review of Pike's two western expeditions to determine if he and his men were entitled to extra compensation as were Lewis and Clark. Also, further mention is made of the same affair in the 29 Cong., 1 sess., *Sen. Exec. Doc.*

IV, No. 66, this time regarding an effort to determine whether Pike's widow was entitled to a pension in lieu of her husband's services in 1805–1807.

A chronological listing of General Pike's assignments, ranks, and promotions in the United States Army is found in F. B. Heitman's *Historical Register and Dictionary of the United States Army* (1903). The brief sketch found therein proved invaluable in keeping straight the General's service record, along with those of his father and other officers with whom he was associated.

Another federal document in which Pike is mentioned is *Messages and Papers of the Presidents,* 1789–1897 (1896), edited by James D. Richardson. This publication contains an account of the Mississippi expedition in 1805–1806 as reported by President Jefferson in his annual message to Congress on December 2, 1806.

Information relating to the North American Indians with whom Pike came in contact during his expeditions to the West is found in the following publications by the Smithsonian Institution, Bureau of Ethnology: *Handbook of American Indians North of Mexico* (1910), edited by Frederick Webb Hodge; Waldo Rudolph Wedel, *An Introduction to Pawnee Archeology, Bulletin 112* (1936); and Wedel, *The Direct Historical Approach in Pawnee Archeology, Miscellaneous Collections,* Vol. XCVII, No. 7 (1938).

3. NEWSPAPERS AND MAGAZINES

A number of newspapers were examined for information pertaining to General Pike and the period in which he lived. Few publications are complete before 1812, but one that proved to be a valuable source of information was the Washington *Intelligencer* in the Library of Congress. I made a fairly complete examination of its files for the years 1805 to 1814. Numerous stories about and references to Pike were found therein: Pike's two expeditions to the West; General Wilkinson's activities in the West and Southwest and his relations with Aaron Burr; the Burr conspiracy and the trial which followed; preparations for the War of 1812; conditions in the army; and military campaigns in 1812 and 1813 in which Pike was involved. Also, several columns are devoted to comments, summaries, and reviews of Pike's book. It should likewise be mentioned that part of the materials used in the chapter on the campaign against York, Canada, and the death of General Pike are based upon information obtained from the *Intelligencer*.

The Natchez Weekly *Chronicle,* files of which were found in the Mississippi Department of Archives and History, Jackson, contains many references to Pike, Claiborne, Wilkinson, and others with whom Pike was associated in Louisiana during the years from 1807 to 1813. This paper is particularly critical and suspicious of General Pike because of his long association with the nefarious General Wilkinson.

Other newspapers in which accounts of General Pike's activities in the West were found are: the Kentucky *Gazette* (1807–12, incomplete), in the University of Kentucky Newspaper Collection, Lexington; the Philadelphia *Aurora* (1807–12), in the Library of Congress; the New Orleans *Louisiana Gazette* (1804–13, incomplete), in Howard Memorial Library, New Orleans.

The only magazine that was examined for contemporary accounts of General Pike and the period from 1805 to 1814 was *Niles' Register,* which was published in Philadelphia and complete files of which are now in the Library of Congress. This publication furnished part of the materials relating to the War of 1812, the campaign into Upper Canada in 1813, and the death of General Pike at the Battle of York.

In more recent years several articles about Pike's career and his discovery of the peak in Colorado have appeared in the Denver *Post* and other Colorado newspapers. But these accounts are based upon secondary sources and are of little value to this study.

Two articles in the Lawrenceburg (Indiana) *Press* are worthy of mention: "The Two Zebulon Pikes," in the issue for March 27, 1927, and "Honor the Sacred Grave of Clara Pike," in the issue for October 20, 1927.

4. BOOKS

Among the printed sources dealing with the life and times of Zebulon Montgomery Pike, the most important is Pike's journal of western travels. The original journal was first published in book form in Philadelphia in 1810 and entitled: *An Account of*

Expeditions to the Sources of the Arkansas, La Platte, and Pierre Juan, Rivers; . . . The above work includes the activities performed by Pike from 1805 to 1807. A copy of the first American edition is now in the Rare Book Room of the Library of Congress. It was set in print without editorial criticism and it is difficult to imagine a more disorderly publication. Consequently, it was of little use to me, inasmuch as better editions were available.

In 1810 an English edition of Pike's journal was published in London, a copy of which is now in the Treasure Room of the University of Oklahoma Library. The English editors shortened the title and succeeded in bringing some order out of the chaos of the American edition. It was this work which I used most frequently in constructing the chapters relating to Pike's two western expeditions.

The best recent, annotated, and most complete edition of Pike's journal and letters is that of Elliott Coues (2 vols. and an atlas, New York, 1895). There is an introductory chapter which contains a biographical sketch of General Pike. The editor has also included several Pike documents which help illuminate the General's career.

A later annotated edition of Pike's journal is that of Milton Quaife, *The Southwestern Expedition of Zebulon Pike* (Chicago, 1925). As the title indicates, the editor has dealt only with the second expedition; however, his work is valuable for its discussion of the Louisiana Territory and its purchase and exploration by the United States.

The most recent work relating to Pike's second expedition is *Zebulon Pike's Arkansas Journal,* edited by Stephen Harding Hart and Archer Butler Hulbert (Denver, 1932). Although the principal part of this study is based upon Pike's journal, the editors have emphasized the geographical aspects of the route taken by Pike through the Southwest. Also, they have vigorously defended Pike's action in the Southwest, protesting the assertion that he was a spy for Wilkinson and Burr.

No comprehensive or scholarly biography of Pike has ever been adequately completed, although mention should be made of the efforts of Henry Whiting. In 1845 his *Life of Pike* appeared in Jared Sparks' *Library of American Biography*, V, 217–314. This work, more than any other printed source, contains information about Pike's career before and after his two western expeditions.

Another biographical sketch of General Pike is found in John M. Nile's *The Life of Oliver Hazard Perry in which is added a Biography of General Pike* (Hartford, 1821). This work not only is brief, but contains many errors about Pike's early life and subsequent career.

Other secondary sources from which background and miscellaneous information were obtained should be given passing mention: James Ripley Jacobs, *The Beginning of the U. S. Army, 1783–1812* (Princeton, 1947); Walter Flavius McCaleb, *The Aaron Burr Conspiracy* (New York, 1936); James Ripley Jacobs, *Tarnished Warrior* (New York, 1938); Royal Ornan Shreve, *The Finished Scoundrel* (Indianapolis, 1933); Robert E. Riegel, *America Moves West* (New York, 1947); Isaac J. Cox, *The Early Exploration of Louisiana* (Cincinnati, 1906); LeRoy R. Hafen and Carl Coke Rister, *Western America* (New York, 1947); Francis McDermott (ed.), *Tixier's Travels on the Osage Prairies* (Norman, Oklahoma, 1940); Harris G. Warren, *The Sword Was Their Passport* (Baton Rouge, 1943); Philip B. Sharpe, *The Rifle in America* (New York, 1938); Francis Bannerman Sons' *Catalogue of Military Goods* (New York, 1938); *The Original Journals of the Lewis and Clark Expedition*, edited by Reuben Gold Thwaites (7 vols. and an atlas, New York, 1904–1905); the journals of George Croghan (Vol. I), André Michaux's *Journal of Travels into Kentucky, 1793–1796* (Vol. III), James Flint's *Letters from America* (Vol. IX), Josiah Gregg's *Commerce of the Prairies* (Vols. XIX and XX), Maximilian, Prince of Wied's *Travels in North America, 1832–34* (Vols. XXII–XXIV), in *Early Western Travels, 1748–1846,* edited by Reuben Gold Thwaites (32 vols., Cleveland, 1904–1906).

And Edwin James, *An Account of an Expedition from Pittsburgh to the Rocky* . . . (3 vols., Philadelphia, 1823), reprinted also as *James's Account of S. H. Long's Expedition, 1819–1820,* in Vols. XIV to XVII, of Thwaites' *Early Western Travels*, mentioned above; H. M. Chittenden, *The American Fur Trade of the Far West* (3 vols., New York, 1902); James Wilkinson, *Memoirs of My Own Times* (3 vols. and an atlas, Philadelphia, 1816); W. P. Webb, *The Great Plains* (New York, 1936); W. C. C. Claiborne, *Official Letter Books* (6 vols., Jackson, Miss., 1917); Edgar McInnis, *Canada, A Political and Social History* (New York, 1947); Ralph Emerson Twitchell, *The Leading Facts of New Mexican History*, I (Cedar Rapids, 1911); Theodore Roosevelt, *The Winning of the West* (4 vols., New York, 1889–96); Albert J. Beveridge, *Life of John Marshall* (4 vols., New York, 1916–19); Paul Leicester Ford (ed.), *Writings of Thomas Jefferson* (10 vols., New York, 1892–99); Gerald W. Johnson, *American Heroes and Hero Worship* (New York, 1943); Ralph Emerson Twitchell (ed.), *The Spanish Archives of New Mexico* . . . (2 vols., Cedar Rapids, 1914); Hubert Howe Bancroft, *History of Arizona and New Mexico* (San Francisco, 1889); Henry Adams, *History of the United States of America During the Second Administration of James Madison* (New York, 1891); A. W. Greely, *Explorers and Travelers* (New York, 1893); and J. Walker McSpadden, *Pioneer Heroes* (New York, 1929).

5. ARTICLES

I read many articles about Pike and the period in which he lived in various historical journals and magazines. Those articles worthy of mention and which contributed some information not found elsewhere are as follows: J. Villasana Haggard, "The Neutral Ground Between Louisiana and Texas, 1806–1821," *The Louisiana Historical Quarterly*, Vol. XXVIII (October, 1945), 1001–28; "Papers of Zebulon Montgomery Pike," *American Historical Review*, Vol. XIII (October, 1908); 798–827; Kyle S. Crichton, "Zeb Pike," *Scribner's Magazine*, Vol. LXXXII (October, 1927), 462–67; LeRoy R. Hafen, "Zebulon Montgomery Pike," *Colorado Magazine*, Vol. XIII (July, 1931), 132–42; "The Pike Exploration Centennial," *Review of Reviews*, Vol. XXXIV, 333–37; John C. Carpenter, "Pike, a Typical American Soldier," *Kansas State Historical Society Quarterly*, Vol. VII, 284–87; "Z. M. Pike's Exploration in Minnesota, 1805–

1806," *Minnesota Historical Society Quarterly*, Vol. I, 540; "A Yankee Captain and Spanish Priest," *Catholic World*, Vol. CXXXVI, 672–79; Isaac J. Cox, "The Louisiana-Texas Frontier," *Texas State Historical Quarterly*, Vol. X (July, 1906), 1–57; Isaac J. Cox, "Opening the Santa Fe Trail," *Missouri Historical Review*, Vol. XXV (October, 1930), 30–66; F. B. Linderman, "Who Was This Soldier Chief," *The American Legion Monthly* (January, 1934), 1 and 56.

And "Colorado," *Time*, Vol. XI (May 10, 1948), 24–25; Leslie Henshaw, "The Aaron Burr Conspiracy in the Ohio Valley," *Ohio Archaeological and Historical Quarterly*, Vol. XXIV (April, 1915), 121–37; Isaac J. Cox, "The Pan-American Policy of Jefferson and Wilkinson," *Mississippi Valley Historical Review*, Vol. I (September, 1914), 212–39; W. R. Shepherd, "Wilkinson and the Beginnings of the Spanish Conspiracy," *American Historical Review*, Vol. IX (April, 1904), 490–506; William J. Backes, "General Zebulon Montgomery Pike, Somerset-Born," *Somerset County Historical Quarterly*, Vol. VIII, 241–50; "Life and Military Service of Zebulon Montgomery Pike," *Collections of the Minnesota Historical Society*, Vol. XII, 220–429; "The Pike Stockade Site and Its Purchase by the State of Colorado," *Colorado Magazine*, Vol. IV, 249–54; Ralph C. Morris, "The Notion of a Great American Desert," *Mississippi Valley Historical Quarterly*, Vol. XIII (September 2, 1926), 190–200.

6. MISCELLANEOUS

Some items of interest were discovered in the following unpublished manuscripts, speeches, and articles: Edwin W. Mills, "Pike's Expedition up the Osage, 1806," MS dated April 29, 1936, in possession of the author; T. R. Hay, "Pike's Journal of Trip up Mississippi, 1805–1806," MS dated September 16, 1946, in possession of the author; Alva Adams, "The Louisiana Purchase and Its First Explorers," an address delivered at Colorado Springs, July 12, 1894, a copy of which is in possession of the author; Ruth Anne Curran, "Biography of Zebulon Montgomery Pike, 1779–1813," M. A. thesis, Washington University, St. Louis, May, 1944.

Index

Adams, Governor Alva, comments on naming of Pike's Peak: 128 f.
Aird, James, Scot trader: 61 ff.
Alancaster, Governor: relations with Pike, 146 ff.; replaced, 154
Albuquerque, New Mexico, Pike visits: 149–50
Allamatuck, New Jersey: 9
Alston, Joseph, contributes to Burr's scheme: 93
American Philosophical Society, backs Michaux expedition: 46
Ark: 50, 51
Arkansas Expedition: authorized by Wilkinson, 52, 101; objectives of, 101 ff.; results of, 146 f.; motives of, 159 f.
Arkansas River: 4; source of, 101; Pike arrives at, 120
Armstrong, General John: made secretary of war, 208; man of action, 209
Arnold, Benedict: Wilkinson compared with, 42; Battle of Saratoga, 48 n.
Arroyo Hondo: 95, 98, 194; boundary, 94

Bastrop lands, purchased by Burr: 94
Bellefontaine: Pike embarked from, 57; Pike child buried at, 108; Pike transferred to, 175
Blennerhasset, Herman, contributes to Burr's scheme: 93
Bloomfield, General Joseph, Pike under command of: 201, 203, 205
Bolton, Dr. Herbert E., finds Pike's lost papers: 169 f.
Breech-dent, Chippewa chief: 85, 86